The
EXPERTS' GUIDE

to

DOING
THINGS
FASTER

The

EXPERTS' GUIDE

to

DOING THINGS FASTER

100 WAYS *TO MAKE* LIFE MORE EFFICIENT

Created by

SAMANTHA ETTUS

CLARKSON POTTER/PUBLISHERS
NEW YORK

Copyright © 2008 by Experts Media LLC

All rights reserved.
Published in the United States by Clarkson Potter/Publishers, an imprint of the
Crown Publishing Group, a division of Random House, Inc., New York.
www.crownpublishing.com
www.clarksonpotter.com

Clarkson N. Potter is a trademark and Potter and colophon are registered
trademarks of Random House, Inc.

See page 340 for contributor credits.

Library of Congress Cataloging-in-Publication Data
Ettus, Samantha.
    The experts' guide to doing things faster : 100 ways to make life more efficient
/ Samantha Ettus.—1st ed.
        p.   cm.
    1. Life skills—Handbooks, manuals, etc.   2. Conduct of life.   I. Title.
HQ2037.E88   2008
640'.43—dc22   2008027695

ISBN 978-0-307-34209-6

Printed in the United States of America

Design by Laura Palese
Illustrations by Catherine Ross

10 9 8 7 6 5 4 3 2 1

First Edition

TO MY LOVES, *Ella* AND *Ruby*,
FOR MAKING EVERY MINUTE WORTH SAVORING

TO MY SOUL MATE, *Mitch*,
FOR MAKING ME STOP TO SMELL THE TULIPS

CONTENTS

CONTENTS

CONTENTS

✳

BODY

✳

CONTENTS

CONTENTS

CONTENTS

INTRODUCTION

Can we win the race against the clock? Whether pleading with our bodies to fall asleep or struggling to cross another item off of our to-do list, we often find ourselves in a losing battle with time.

As someone who is passionate about everything but sitting still, I am always in pursuit of a more efficient life. To find it, I have engaged the nation's leading experts to map an all-out assault on lost time and inefficiency.

While we are not likely to find an extra hour in our day, we can make the most of the twenty-four we have. Do I have to choose between putting the girls to bed and heading to that dinner party? Not if I can avoid traffic and find a parking spot fast once we get there! Do I need to wake up at the crack of dawn? Not if I can speed up my morning routine to get out the door faster. Every extra minute we can squeeze out of life's requirements adds a minute to life's joys.

To narrow down the abundance of possible topics, I talked to efficiency seekers across the country to find out where they needed speed. The 100 most popular suggestions are covered in these pages—from getting through airport security to speeding up your metabolism.

The 100 carefully selected experts in these pages represent the most experienced and creative minds in the world. Each expert has written his or her own chapter specifically for this book, sharing his or her talent, perspective, and expertise as efficiently as possible.

In a few short minutes you will learn to increase your gas mileage, reduce credit card debt, and bake a cake—all in a flash.

Neil Strauss, the world's greatest pickup artist, shares his secrets to making a winning first impression. If his advice works out for you, perhaps you'll need tips on planning a wedding fast. Not to worry—Vegas's premier wedding planner Tory L. Cooper tells you how. If it is inspiration you seek, I tapped into the mind of Richard Bolles, bestselling author of *What Color Is Your Parachute?*, to help you find your calling. If that involves starting a business, Sir Richard Branson will tell you how to get a loan without delay. Moving? Real estate maven Barbara Corcoran will help you sell your home in record time, and Oprah's favorite event planner, Colin Cowie, will have you whipping up a dinner party in celebration.

Seizing more from life isn't just about saving time—it's about using time to our advantage. Whether overcoming guilt, burying the hatchet, or recovering from a breakup, speed delivers rewards of its own. And when it comes to the mind, whether learning to relax or forming opinions, doing things faster often involves doing things slower.

You are likely pressed for time, so I have organized the book by the following categories so that you can efficiently find what matters to you most.

HOME: from washing dishes to finding a lost object

WORK: from making your computer run faster to achieving your goals

MIND: from doing math in your head to unleashing your creativity

BODY: from running to dressing slimmer

LOVE: from building a great relationship to getting pregnant

PLEASURE: from getting in a good mood to making friends

TRAVEL: from packing to navigating a new city

FUTURE: from going green to building wealth

In the race against time, you are no longer on your own. Welcome to a faster and fuller life.

HOME

–1–
SELL A HOME

BARBARA CORCORAN

Barbara Corcoran is the founder of The Corcoran Group.
She is the host of The Millionaire Inside *on CNBC and
the author of two books, including* If You Don't Have Big
Breasts, Put Ribbons on Your Pigtails.

The key to selling a home fast is to price it right. You could spend all the money in the world fixing up and marketing your house, but the wrong price on the right house will guarantee you it won't sell.

Before you set the price, you've got to walk in the shoes of a buyer. Start by shopping online for local houses similar to yours. If your house has four bedrooms, a brand-new kitchen, and no backyard, that's exactly what you should shop for. Don't be tempted to look at houses that have features yours doesn't, as that's the kind of stinkin' thinkin' that starts sellers down the road to overpricing. It really *does* make a difference that your house has only three baths when the other has four.

Invite three competitive brokers to see your home and estimate its value. Ask them, "What would I have to price my home at if I wanted to sell it in thirty days?" This is the surefire way to get the brokers' gut reaction based on what's happening in the market right now. Even the best brokers feel pressured to flatter the seller when asked to price a home, but the truth is the broker who gives the lowest price is always right.

Take out your list of the comparable homes you found online and pick out the five least expensive. Average those with the three broker estimates for your house. Now price your home 5 percent lower than the number you get. I know, you think I'm crazy. I'm not. Don't ever be afraid of underpricing your home, because market forces immediately correct an underpriced property. It's called a bidding war, and you'll be smiling when it starts.

Spend a couple of weekends visiting neighborhood open houses. You'll get an instant education in what *not* to do when marketing your own home. You'll see that the most important change to make is to get rid of all your clutter. Stuff makes houses look smaller and buyers can't see past clutter to imagine themselves living there. Pack or store two-thirds of your things, including your furniture.

People love light and they're willing to pay for it. After location, the top reason buyers choose a particular home is light. Take down your drapes, wash your windows, and paint your walls a soft white. Trim back the bushes, replace your lamp shades, and install high-wattage bulbs.

Next, scrub your house clean. Make it spotless. People buy with their noses, too, so eliminate all odors that accumulate from smoking, old clothing, and kitty litter. Before the first open house, open all your windows for a full eight hours. No one wants to move into *your* bathroom, so freshen it with a new shower curtain and toilet seat, and buy some new towels.

It rarely pays to renovate your kitchen, but consider painting or replacing your cabinet fronts instead or adding a new countertop. Sometimes simply updating the cabinet knobs and drawer pulls makes all the difference.

Don't overlook the front yard and entryway. From my years showing properties, I'm convinced that buyers decide if they're going to buy your house within the first eight seconds of seeing it. So set your stopwatch, get out of your car, and register what you see in the first eight seconds. Chances are some yard work awaits you. Paint your door and trim, and check to make sure your doorbell works.

Now that you're ready to rock 'n' roll, it's picture time. Rent a professional camera with a wide-angle lens and take photos on a sunny day. The wide-angle lens will make your house and property look bigger. Today, one in three houses are advertised online, and people skip properties with poor pictures. Post at least six good house photos, inside and outside, online.

Finally, hire yourself a killer broker to sell your home. Eighty percent of all commissions are earned by the top 10 percent of agents out there. You want one of those agents working for you. To find the right one, call your local real estate office and ask the sales manager for his or her personal recommendation. And don't be cheap—don't try to negotiate their commission. If you've hired the right broker, you'll get much more than your money's worth.

–2–

BUY A HOUSE

RICHARD C. DAVIS

Richard C. Davis is president, CEO, and founder of Trademark Properties in Charleston, South Carolina. He was the creator and star of the reality show Flip This House *on A&E and is now the creator and star of* The Real Deal *on TLC.*

egardless of what you may have read about the housing market, the first thing you need to understand is that *now* is always a good time to buy a home. Whether it be your first or last house, homeownership still is and always will be the American Dream. Don't put it off any longer; you may have missed a great opportunity while reading this chapter, so let's GET IN, GET you OUT looking, and GO GET you into a home! Take a Dramamine if you don't like speed, 'cause here we go:

TIME IS MONEY

Whether it is a buyer's market or a seller's market, time is always money when it comes to securing a deal on a home. So when you decide to look, you need to make it a priority and invest the time and energy you would if you knew this was going to be the biggest financial decision you will ever make—because chances are it could be. Treat your search as a full-time job until you are done. If you want to do it right, start looking around, surf the Internet, and educate yourself on the available product by reading real estate publications before you ever step foot in the first house.

TEAMWORK MAKES THE "AMERICAN DREAM" WORK

Don't be a cheapskate and try to make one of the biggest investment decisions of your life without first putting together your own personal "dream team." The first thing you want to do is hire a realtor, specifically a "buyer's broker." He or she will use all his or her insight to find you the property that best meets your needs, and will negotiate the best deal possible on your behalf. Your broker will also serve as a great resource in helping you fill out the rest of your team.

YOUR DREAM TEAM:

1. REALTOR/BUYER'S BROKER: helps you find your home on dreamy terms
2. INSPECTOR: makes sure you get what you bargained for
3. CONTRACTOR: fixes what your inspector finds unsatisfactory
4. LENDER: your partner in the dream
5. APPRAISER: checks your realtor's homework
6. CLOSING ATTORNEY: puts the deed in your name
7. LOCKSMITH: changes the locks so you can rest assured that the previous owner's plumber, uncle, or nosy neighbor doesn't use his spare key to drop in unexpectedly

The number-one rule in the purchasing process is to remove all emotions from your decision making. It is not personal taste that matters most. Rather, it's the best deal—regardless of appearance—that wins out. When finding a home, you can satisfy both your personal taste and your desire for a great deal if you follow this strategy:

Rank potential properties based on your personal taste, putting price aside for the moment. Then ask your realtor to rank the ten best deals on the market that match your needs based on location, school district, number of bedrooms, number of bathrooms, square footage, and any other special requirements you may have. You will be amazed at how quickly your fifth choice based on curb appeal becomes your all-time favorite when you find the owner will take a deep discount, while your former top choice drops to the bottom of the pack when the owner won't budge even a dollar from her asking price.

After you rank the properties, make offers on at least three simultaneously. If one of your first offers is accepted, be alarmed and dig deeper; either your buyer's agent left something on the table, or what looks "too good to be true" probably is. This is where the rest of your team comes into play—to ensure that you make a great decision that you will be happy with for years to come. After you have a property under contract, you must hire an inspector to check the condition of the home and make sure everything is in working order so there are no surprises after the closing.

Now, take your checklist, pack it away, and pat yourself on the back. You just took the fast track to the American Dream—homeownership!

—3—

REMODEL

LAURA MEYER

Laura Meyer is an attorney and the coauthor of Remodel
This! A Woman's Guide to Planning and
Surviving the Madness of a Home Renovation.
She is the home columnist for Dame *magazine.*

W hen it comes to remodeling, the same themes come up in every conversation: "I just can't get my contractor to finish up those last few things," or "It was supposed to be a six-month project and now it's going on a year." Here's how to avoid a similar fate:

PLAN, PLAN, PLAN

Many people dive into their projects without planning the details in advance, not realizing that while advanced planning may delay the start of work, even the most rudimentary of plans can make things go a whole lot faster and more smoothly. Time is saved when the professionals have a solid handle on your vision, so start planning early. Thumb through design magazines, surf the Net, and cut or print out pictures that capture your vision.

Visit stores and showrooms and get copies of catalogs. Show what you've collected to your contractor, designer, or architect. Armed with this information, architects require less time to devise satisfactory plans and contractors less time to provide accurate bids. Additionally, materials can then be ordered sooner so that the project doesn't get delayed as a result of long lead times.

CHOOSE YOUR GENERAL CONTRACTOR WISELY

Nobody on your team is more essential than your general contractor (GC). Hiring the right GC is the most important thing you can do to set your remodel up for success. Conversely, hiring the wrong person can translate into all kinds of problems and delays—not the least of which can be caused by having to fire him!

Of course, you want to hire someone who is competent, reliable, and trustworthy, but also someone with whom you have a good rapport. Don't fall for the first contractor you meet just because he seems nice. Instead, check your candidates out thoroughly:

- **MAKE SURE HE HAS THE RIGHT CREDENTIALS.** Make sure the GC is licensed (most states require it). Check out his standing with your state's licensing board and contact your local Better Business Bureau for records of complaints.

- **MEET HIS PAST CLIENTS.** GCs should give you references and you should contact them. Ask a lot of questions. Find out what went right and what went wrong. Inquire whether their project was completed on time, and if not, why. Visit other homes the GC has remodeled to check out his work.

- **MAKE SURE HE HAS TIME FOR YOUR JOB.** Good contractors are in demand and often juggle numerous projects. Make sure he has time for you and can make your job a priority.

GET IT IN WRITING

Whether your project is big or small, get your agreement in writing. You'll be vulnerable to all sorts of problems without a clear and thorough contract. Include a payment schedule tied to completion of the various stages of the project. The contractor's bids (including a breakdown of prices) should be attached and made part of the contract. If your project is large, have a real estate lawyer take a look at the contract.

Identify a date for substantial completion in the contract. Without that your project could last forever. On the other hand, you don't want your contractor to commit to a date that is too early for the project to be done well, as this may cause him to cut corners in an effort to speed things up. This is where communication with the contractor is key.

HAVE WEEKLY MEETINGS

Once the work starts, make sure you stay on top of your contractor's progress through weekly meetings. If you are not living in the home during the remodel, go to the job site regularly and make sure the workers are there when they should be.

DON'T MAKE THE FINAL PAYMENT UNTIL ALL WORK IS DONE

One of the most common complaints I hear is that it's impossible to get the contractor to finish up even if he was great for most of the job. Give him an incentive and don't make that last payment until every single thing has been completed.

—4—

REDECORATE

EVETTE RIOS

Evette Rios is a featured regular decorating and crafts "buddy" on The Rachael Ray Show *and a correspondent for* The G Word, *on Discovery Network's Planet Green channel. She works as an interior designer for a number of private clients.*

A newly redecorated home can help you spend more time with your family, sleep better, work harder, and feel sexier. But everything takes two and a half times longer than you think it will and going through the process can leave you feeling uprooted. So here are some tips for fast, fun redecorating.

STEP BY STEP

Start with one area. Go room by room. Focus your attention carefully, or you risk burning out with your space half-finished. Redoing a whole home is a full-time job, so don't expect to do it in a weekend. Divide your project into manageable chunks and you'll have fun, stay sane, and achieve fantastic results efficiently.

USE WHAT YOU HAVE

Use what you've got when possible. This will save time, money, and the earth. Some of your existing pieces won't jive with your new decor, but things you've had for years might be of higher quality than much of the store-bought stuff you can get now. This is especially true of hardwood furniture. Embrace cushions, slipcovers, and throw pillows to save time and money while really giving old furniture a new look.

EDUCATE YOUR EYES

Think of yourself as the artist of your home. The more you strive to expand your vision as you go through your everyday life, the more your space will be inspired and the quicker you will finish. Spend a few hours in a bookstore or the library, and look at as many rooms as you can. Flip through home magazines and design books and explore websites focused on interiors. Create a scrapbook and capture digital photographs of images you love to streamline your shopping process later.

With educated eyes, every outing becomes a subconscious shopping trip. You may stumble upon that perfect piece while running errands or spot it at a local yard sale—but you'll notice it only if you have been thinking ahead. Like a Boy Scout, the quick and efficient redecorator must always be prepared.

MUST-HAVE TOOLS

MEASURING TAPE: Measure your entire space before you do any shopping. Nothing is more satisfying than finding the right fit for that oddly-sized nook, or more frustrating than finding your dream sofa won't fit through the door unless you saw the legs off.

FOLDER OR BINDER: Fill this with images of the stuff you have and the stuff you like. If you are using a binder, insert sheet protectors so that you can keep fabric and wallpaper samples organized and within your reach.

PAINT FANDEX: These are books with swatches of paint colors. You can get them from your neighborhood paint store. Invaluable! And not just for paint. Use for matching colors on everything from rugs to sofa fabric.

FURNITURE GLIDES: Enlist a friend to tuck these under your larger pieces and you'll be able to rearrange them with ease, even completely unassisted. This will save you time, frustration, and lower-back pain. Try moving the larger pieces first—they are the toughest to work around.

ASK, ASK, ASK

When you're in a tight time frame, always make sure to ask the salesperson what is in stock before you fall in love with anything. Otherwise, be prepared to wait the dreaded four to ten weeks for delivery. And forget about ordering anything custom—unless you are prepared to wait, make seventeen phone calls to find out why you have been waiting so long, and then wait some more.

BE FLEXIBLE

It's great to know what you want, but if you need to get things done in a pinch you'll need to be open to other options. The marble-top table you had your sights set on isn't in stock? Go for glass, and save your time and creative energy to spend elsewhere.

TRUST YOUR INSTINCTS

Design gurus put so much emphasis on rules, but every time they cleverly break one they are lauded. Break the rules as often as you want but do try to keep things comfortable. Certain dimensions have become standard because they are the most comfortable for an averaged-scaled human, so you don't want to deviate too much from those guidelines.

—5—
TACKLE YOUR TO-DO LIST

KATE GOSSELIN

Kate Gosselin manages a family of ten. Along with her husband, Jon; twins, Cara and Madelyn; and sextuplets, Alexis, Aaden, Collin, Leah, Hannah, and Joel, she is the star of Jon & Kate Plus 8 *on TLC and is the author of* Multiple Bles8ings.

S mall army in your house or not, it can be difficult to respond to life's curveballs. It could be a last-minute meeting, the kids acting out, or an overwhelming colleague; life has a way of turning an everyday situation into an extraordinary adventure. Maintaining a high level of organization helps any person or household—supersized or otherwise—run efficiently. Whether you're planning a picnic for ten, a hike in the woods, or just a quick trip to the mall, plan ahead with a to-do list. Let's start with one now.

1. TAKE A DEEP BREATH. Set aside some quiet time to think about the big picture. Grab a cup of coffee in the morning before your hectic day begins and think about how you would like the day to unfold. Think through the best-case scenario and then, God forbid, the worst-case scenario. This will help you visualize the day's activities and what it will take to get things done. Taking a moment or two to clear your mind will go a long way as you start on any task.

2. WRITE IT DOWN. No one has the memory of an elephant. Buy a small notebook or, if you prefer, use your handheld device to type out your list. Outline the main groups of activities or events to accomplish. Start with a no-brainer, like grocery shopping, and then move on to other activities, such as meals for the week or which bills have to be paid. Grouping the main activities in your life creates natural categories for your to-do lists.

3. PRIORITIZE. Once the categories are outlined, prioritize the list. Highlight the time-sensitive items that must get done immediately and start with those.

4. CLEAN THE SLATE. Keep a constant running list of to-dos in each category and then cross things off as they are completed. If you feel overwhelmed when you look at a growing list with only a few items scratched off, reward yourself by starting a new list and transfer the yet-to-be-completed items. Do this on a daily or weekly basis, depending on how big the list becomes. This provides a sense of accomplishment, and sometimes a fresh perspective.

5. DEVELOP A ROUTINE. A routine helps everyone by removing the guesswork and a lot of frustration. Having a schedule provides the structure to get the things on your to-do list done, which helps to manage the unpredictable nature of life.

6. PREPARE FOR OUTINGS. If you prepare in advance, it will be easier to live in the moment when you get to your destination.

7. INVOLVE YOUR SUPPORT NETWORK. Don't be a martyr! Too often in life, we feel as if we have to take on everything ourselves. One efficient aspect of having a to-do list is that you can proactively determine where you can involve other people in your life. If you have children, invite them to join you for family chores as well as the fun times. This helps to provide family unity while instilling a strong sense of independence and responsibility. If you have roommates, make Saturday cleaning day a friendly affair. If you have colleagues, split up your responsibilities. Including others gets the job done faster, eases stress, and provides time for bonding amid hectic schedules.

8. REWARD YOUR TEAM. On days when your life seems filled with to-dos, remember to count your blessings, big or small. Take a moment to feel gratitude for all that is positive in your life and don't forget to reward your helpers for their assistance and kindness, too. This will make tackling tasks more enjoyable and it makes them even more likely to want to help you again next time.

—6—

CLEAN YOUR HOME

MARY LOUISE STARKEY

Mary Louise Starkey, a.k.a. The First Lady of Service, is the founder and president of The Starkey International Institute for Household Management in Denver, Colorado. She is credited with coining the term "Household Manager."

efore you can begin to housekeep, you must determine what your family means by "clean." The term "clean" can refer not only to how a home looks but also to how it feels. Your own physical and emotional housekeeping standards may be allergy-motivated and require a dust-free environment, or perhaps you'd like your home to meet the conventions of your grandmother, who scrubbed floors on her hands and knees. Goals for some may be child-friendly; clean, but cluttered; comfortably clean; or sort of clean. Others may establish rules that require a specific place for everything in the home. If you have pets or teens who rule the home, your standards might allow for a bit of dirt and mess, as squeaky clean is simply not a priority.

Depending on your conventions, you may need to clean your entire home each week. This is the most common mentality and keeps the home "clean" and orderly for about five full days. The number of cleanable square feet determines, naturally, the amount of time necessary to clean a home. On average, it takes one hour to clean 500 square feet. Of course, higher standards require more time, but there are some tricks of the trade you can employ to speed things up without missing a spot.

Begin by developing a housekeeping plan that utilizes Zoning and Task Sheets:

Zoning is the process of designating physical areas of function within the home according to flow and determining where the heavy traffic areas are as people move from one part of the home to another. Heavy flow will dictate which rooms need the most attention—more traffic flow translates to more frequent use, and sometimes more time dedicated to cleaning. Visually define your home and create your zones by referencing either architectural drawings or your own handy sketches.

Task Sheets organize and list appropriate duties to be accomplished in each room or area within a zone. Tasks may include dusting, vacuuming, detailing the car, or changing the air filters, and may be designated for repeat daily, weekly, monthly, or even yearly. In addition, it helps to:

- Define how you want things to be cleaned
- Determine and always keep stocked appropriate cleaning products and tools for each task in each zone

To clean properly and efficiently you must know exactly how long it takes to clean the entire home. So clean it yourself before you get your family or housekeeper (if you're lucky) to help you clean in the future. Learn your home's cleaning issues, what products you want used for each surface, and which zones the family uses most often.

SAMPLE LIVING ROOM WEEKLY TASK SHEET

Area	Time	Description of Work	Product
Entire room	1 min.	Straighten and put items in proper locations.	
Ceiling light fixtures	1 min.	Dust from the top down, inside and out, including lightbulbs.	Ostrich feather duster
Wall molding, doors	2 min.	Dust from the top down. Check for spots or fingerprints. Clean as necessary.	Ostrich feather duster, all-purpose cleaner, cleaning cloth
Furniture and flat surfaces	2 min.	Dust from the top down, inside and out, starting from the back corner of the room, then from the sides to the center.	Ostrich feather duster
Glass surfaces	5 min.	Clean and polish, checking for streaks.	Glass cleaner and lint-free cloth
Upholstered furniture	4 min.	Vacuum surfaces and underneath cushions using upholstery attachment. Fluff and replace pillows.	Vacuum
Antique rug	10 min.	Vacuum with the nap of the rug, avoiding fringe. Brush fringe to lie flat and straight.	Vacuum, carpet brush
	5 min.	Take cleaning products and trash with you when finished.	

Total time: 30 minutes

Be sure to organize tasks within each area according to a logical flow so that precious time is not wasted.

This method is the best way to keep track of what housekeeping is really being accomplished in your home. If you fall behind in the duties on your Task Sheet, note them and adjust the time, the frequency, or even the person completing them. It's a process, but implementing this system will have you housekeeping better and faster than anyone!

–7–

DO LAUNDRY

LUCINDA OTTUSCH

Lucinda Ottusch is a senior home economist and fabric care specialist for the Whirlpool Institute of Fabric Science. Ottusch has spent the last ten years researching the washing and drying process to determine the most effective ways to care for fabrics.

The quickest way to do laundry is to do it right the first time. Yet many people struggle to get the results they desire, partially because they follow more traditional "old school" laundry methods. Instead, try these more efficient "new school" approaches:

ORGANIZING

OLD SCHOOL: You drag your clothes to an unorganized laundry room and end up sorting, folding, and treating laundry all over the house, from beds to living rooms. Recent research found that 80 percent of consumers lack space and storage to perform laundry tasks.
NEW SCHOOL: Make laundry more tolerable by transforming your laundry room into a livable, productive work space.

- Stock your laundry room with bins, laundry tools, and hangers to suit every fabric need.

- Install a system with work surfaces for sorting and folding, and storage towers to hold bulk detergents, stain sticks, and fabric softener sheets.

- Use color-coded baskets to sort darks, lights, and whites.

STAINS

OLD SCHOOL: You rub stains with a stain fighter and toss into the wash.

NEW SCHOOL: Blot stains, don't rub, and tackle them from the inside out as soon as possible.

- Place the stained area facedown on a clean paper towel, then apply stain remover to the underside of the garment to loosen the stain.

- Keep a laminated cheat sheet handy with stain-removal tricks.

DETERGENTS

OLD SCHOOL: You use one detergent for all loads, no matter the nature of the stain, size, or fabric.

NEW SCHOOL: Use the right detergent for the right appliance and load.

- Just as dish soap should not be used in a dishwasher, many washing machines require specially formulated detergents. For example, when used in high-efficiency (HE) machines, traditional detergents can create excess suds, which can lead to the development of odor-causing residue like body oils, dirt, and grime. Excess suds cause HE machines to use additional water and extend cycle length, costing time and money.

- In low-temperature cycles use detergents designed for cold water. Traditional detergents do not dissolve well in cold water and may streak clothing.

WASHING

OLD SCHOOL: You limit your cycles to one tried-and-true favorite setting.

NEW SCHOOL: Make the most of your varied temperature and feature options on your washing machine.

- Many machines feature a variety of innovative cycles to do the work for you. Manufacturers equip machines with sensors to determine the load size, which saves time and maintains eco-efficiency.

- Water temperature is important to keep whites bright and prevent dulling of darks. Soils like sweat and body oils are best removed in hot water, while colors may require colder temperatures to prevent pigment loss. If fabrics are discolored or gray, use higher temperatures.

DRYING

OLD SCHOOL: You wait for the dry cycle to finish before starting a new load.

NEW SCHOOL: Do multiple loads in a row, so the dryer does not lose heat between loads, boosting energy savings.

- If clothes need a quick refresh, toss a damp towel in the load to loosen wrinkles.

Laundry may not be your favorite chore, but streamlining the process will help you get the job done faster and improve your results.

–8–

IRON

BARBARA ZAGNONI

Barbara Zagnoni, a.k.a. The Queen of Steam, is the consumer education director for Rowenta, Inc., the leading manufacturer of high-end irons. She appears regularly on QVC on behalf of Rowenta.

What's the quickest way to expertly iron an uncooperative shirt? How do you get your pants looking crisp when you need to be at that big event in just fifteen minutes? Questions like these seem pretty minor until you're the one facing them. The following tips will help you learn how to take the chore out of ironing.

THE RIGHT TOOL FOR THE JOB

Acquiring a suitable iron is your first big step. A good iron has a stainless steel soleplate (it's the most durable and offers the best glidability), the ability to make vertical steam, and an accurate thermostat. Choose an iron with high wattage (1400 to 1800 watts), which will keep the iron hot without leaking and spitting.

A FEW SIMPLE TIPS

If you don't follow the proper steps in order, you will actually make your garment more wrinkled than when you started, a surefire way to become frustrated and regret not having taken your item to a professional. And before you do anything else, make sure to place the iron on the proper setting for the fabric you are ironing. For example, for cotton and linen, set the iron at its highest setting for maximum heat and steam.

SHIRTS

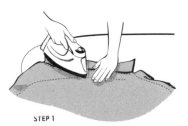

STEP 1

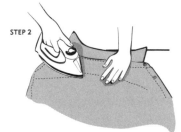

STEP 2

STEP 1

Start with the underside of the collar. Iron from the center to avoid creasing. Flip and repeat on the other side.

STEP 2

Hook one shoulder over the round tip of the ironing board. Start at the yoke (where the collar meets the shoulder) and move to the center of the back. Repeat with the other shoulder.

STEP 3

STEP 3
Lay one sleeve flat with the buttons or cuff link holes facing up. Iron the inside of the cuff. Flip and iron the outside of the cuff. Then iron into the sleeve, starting on the button side. Repeat with the other sleeve.

STEP 4

STEP 4
Iron one side of the front of the shirt first and then move to the back. Finish by ironing the remaining front panel. Be careful to iron between the buttons and not over them, which can cause the buttons to break.

PANTS

STEP 1
Flip the pockets to the outside and lay them flat to iron. (If the pocket material is different than that of the pants, adjust the temperature setting down a bit.) If the iron sticks at all, your temperature is too high.

STEP 2
Turn the pockets right side out. Hook the waistband over the point of the ironing board. Rotate the pants around the board as you iron. Iron gently over the pocket areas to avoid creases.

STEP 3
Place one leg atop the other. Align the inseams. Fold back the top of the leg. Iron the inside of the leg from the bottom to the crotch.

Flip and iron the outside of the leg. Fold back and repeat these steps with the other leg. For pants without creases, iron near the legs' edges, but not over them.

STEP 4

To create a crease along the front of the pants, hold the iron a few inches from the leg and direct a burst of steam toward its edge. Then iron, using a spray of cool mist if necessary.

OTHER IRONING TIPS

- TO AVOID WRINKLES AFTER IRONING: Wearing a garment immediately after ironing can cause new wrinkles to form. To protect against wrinkles, let the garment hang for about five minutes after it has been ironed. This enables it to set, creating a sharp, pressed look that lasts longer.

- TO USE SPRAY STARCH: Many people like the extra crispness that starch can provide, particularly with shirts. To obtain that look, spray a small amount of starch on the shirt, roll the shirt into a ball, and wait thirty seconds before pressing.

- TO REMOVE SOLEPLATE BUILDUP: Soleplate buildup can be caused by a variety of things (starch, fabric softener, hard-water mineral deposits, even dust). If your soleplate gets dirty, you can clean it quickly and easily with a wax-based hot iron cleaner. Put a dime-sized drop of the cleaner on a towel and move the hot iron across it. The buildup will thereby be transferred to the towel. If the soleplate is very dirty, you may need to repeat this step. When finished, buff the iron with an old cloth or towel to ensure that it is completely clean.

—9—

ORGANIZE YOUR CLOSET

JOHN TROSKO

*John Trosko is president of OrganizingLA, a Los Angeles–
based professional organizing and lifestyle management
company. He is president of the National Association of
Professional Organizers, Los Angeles Chapter.*

When properly ordered, your closet can save you time. Here are the seven successful *P* strategies for optimizing your closet.

1. PURPOSE

Avoid the fast and the furious. Organizing your closet should be a continual practice, not a one-time episode. Don't try to carry out the entire job in one day or you'll burn out. Plan a manageable amount of time daily to tackle the myriad details inside. Keep your mind on a reward for you to enjoy when you complete your organizing project (e.g., a special trip to the manicurist, a favorite meal, or tickets to a ball game).

2. PULL OUT

There are dozens of ways to organize a closet; the right way is your way. If you're crunched for space, it doesn't make sense to pull everything out all over the bedroom. Split your organizing into small tasks: floor, shoes and shoe cubbies, top and bottom shelves, middle shelves, closet rods, drawers, cabinets, mysterious treasure boxes. While you move throughout the closet, categorize similar items together. Dust, vacuum, and wipe all surfaces to give you a clean slate.

3. PURGE

Successful closet organizing requires tough choices about what flatters your best assets and what doesn't. Forecast what your life will hold for you in the next year. Everything in your closet should have a purpose for today and tomorrow, not yesterday. Set up a series of bins or bags to sort out items to keep, donate, trash, mend/repair (for those long-neglected fixes), give away (maternity clothes to your sister), recycle (wire hangers, dry cleaning bags, paper, etc.), and miscellaneous projects. Along the way you'll find objects that need to be relocated elsewhere in your home (so add a bin for that, too). Warning: Do not allow these relocations to distract you. Stay with the closet. As an extra shot in the arm, call in a trusted friend who can coach you through the "How do I look?" phase. Tripping down memory lane will be easier if you know your unused items will be more useful to a charity.

4. PURCHASE

Carry out all the projects and make a shopping list for needs that have emerged from your newly slimmed-down wardrobe. Every closet requires the following organizing products: clothes hamper (for both laundry and dry cleaning), mesh bag (for hand-washing), shelf dividers (so sweaters, pants, and T-shirts don't tumble), wastebasket, sewing kit, jars (for buttons, collar stays, and clothing tags), an open basket (for cell phone, coins, and wallet), and several large storage containers (for rotating out-of-season clothing). Measure your shelves before you shop to avoid time-consuming returns.

5. PUT IN

Before loading your life back into the space, assign a counter or shelf to act as a temporary way station to dump daily stuff you'll put away later. Second, find a permanent home for your everyday purse, briefcase, messenger bag, or gym bag. Third, organize your clothes according to how you use them. Anything you wear repeatedly should be within effortless grasp, and rarely used items go on a higher shelf or another out-of-the-way spot. Place scarves, belts, hats, and jewelry on or in decorative hooks and baskets.

6. PRIMP

Once your purging and purchasing have taken place, you may choose to invest in a few optional decorative touches if time permits. To brighten a wardrobe, repaint the closet a clean, crisp white and replace lights with higher-wattage bulbs. Arrange items by hanging length, season, type, and color. Apply labels to mark your bins to avoid uncertainty about where things go. Install a full-length mirror on the back of the door. Buy matching hangers to unify the visual look of the space.

7. PROCESS

Organizing your closet is like giving it a Botox injection. The change may be only visual and cosmetic. Follow the habit of tidying everyday disorder to maintain your organized grandeur. The organization is the inner beauty. I find the best time to tidy is just prior to laundry day or during seasonal changes—when a closet is somewhat emptier and you have space to move around.

Remember, a disorganized closet is not a life sentence. Follow these strategies and you'll soon be walking into your walk-in.

–10–
SORT MAIL

PETER WALSH

> *Peter Walsh is the professional organizer on TLC's*
> Clean Sweep *and the author of three books, including*
> It's All Too Much: An Easy Plan for Living a Richer
> Life with Less Stuff. *He is the host of* The Peter Walsh
> Show *on Oprah & Friends radio network.*

The average American receives close to fifty thousand pieces of mail during his or her lifetime—of which about a third is junk mail. Like an endless flood, the mail keeps coming. Sometimes it seems that all we can do is throw our hands in the air in despair and accept the fact that we will drown in the endless tide of paperwork. However, with these simple steps, the mail can be conquered and—come hail, sleet, or snow—you can be on top of it once and for all.

1. Don't let the mail pile up—commit to sorting and dealing with it every day. Taking care of the mail as part of your daily routine is a huge step toward getting on top of it.

2. Streamline the mail handling process by establishing a mail station in your home or office—this will be the one location where

you place and sort all your mail. Put a couple of trays or bins in this area, as well as a trash can and shredder. Sort the mail immediately and try to handle each piece only once: throw it out, file it, or act on it. Don't procrastinate when it comes to this daily task.

3. Place a pin board close to the mail station. Pin upcoming events, reminders, or invitations to the board so you can clearly and quickly see what commitments you have. Regularly remove outdated items.

4. Keep a bin handy for all those magazines and catalogs you don't want or need. Immediately throw into the bin any mail items in which you have no interest. When the bin is full, recycle the contents.

5. Junk mail is your enemy. Do not let it take up residence in your home—ever! Immediately shred all junk mail, including anything that may contain your credit card numbers, Social Security number, or other sensitive personal information, to avoid any problems with identity theft.

6. Decrease the amount of mail coming into your home by getting your name off junk-mail lists. Phone 1-888-5OPT OUT (1-888-567-8688) to have your name removed from lists that send those annoying credit card offers. Likewise, log on to www.catalog choice.org to remove your name from lists that stuff your mailbox with unwanted catalogs.

7. Use technology to your advantage by paying as many bills as you can online. Not only will this reduce the volume of paper you have to deal with, but it will also save you time and energy.

8. Keep all bills that need to be paid in a separate tray or bin at the mail station. Also keep on hand all necessary bill-paying items—stamps, envelopes, your checkbook, etc. During the last week of every month go through all bills that need to be paid. This

routine will help you avoid late payments and manage your finances better.

9. If you're uncomfortable with discarding paid bills, invest in a twelve-month expanding file. Place the stubs for all paid bills into the month in which they're paid. If at the end of twelve months you haven't needed to look at the paid bills, it's unlikely you ever will, so shred them.

10. Establish a good filing system. File only those items that you need to keep. Talk to your accountant or a financial consultant to be sure of what documents you must retain for tax purposes.

Remember: The mail is your friend—but only if you control it. Establishing a single mail center in your home and sticking to a clear mail routine will solve your mail problem.

–11–

FILE

KATHY PEEL

Kathy Peel, a.k.a. America's Family Manager, is the founder and CEO of Family Manager Coaching. She has written nineteen books, which have sold more than 2 million copies. She is AOL's Family and Kids coach.

Paper clutter moves in and multiplies, and before you know it you're wasting time searching through piles for important information. If you can't envision having a free day in the next five years, you can conquer paper clutter a little bit at a time in just a few minutes here or a half hour there.

To keep paper from proliferating, follow this simple eight-step excavation plan. Dig in and start digging out.

1. Put all the papers you need to deal with or file in one place. Get a wastebasket, a recycle box, file folders, labels, pens, and a stapler.

2. Turn a pile of papers over before you go through them, so that the oldest papers are on top. You'll see progress faster because typically you can throw away many of the older documents.

3. Start with the first paper: Decide if it's valuable and necessary.

If not, toss or recycle it. (See below for ideas on what to toss.) If it's worth keeping, move to step 4.

4. Choose a file heading for the paper, label a folder appropriately, and file the paper in the corresponding folder.

5. If there are two or more papers associated with the topic you're dealing with, staple the papers together. Don't use paper clips; they get caught on each other and fall off easily.

6. Pick up the next piece of paper and follow the same procedure, except to file it in the appropriate file if you've already created one. Consolidate as much as you can.

7. When you've finished with all of your papers, sort the files according to the seven "Departments" explained below, then alphabetize the files within each department. Place files in a file drawer or carton.

8. Purge regularly. Each time you refer to a file, thumb through it and discard any papers that are no longer necessary.

DEPARTMENTS

All of the tasks and responsibilities that come with running your home, family, and personal life can be better managed when categorized in seven departments and supervised accordingly. When setting up your filing system, create a section for each of these:

- **HOME AND PROPERTY:** Overseeing the maintenance and care of all tangible assets, including your belongings, your home and its surroundings, and your vehicles. Examples of papers to be filed in this department are decorating ideas, trash collection, auto information, dream house pictures and plans, gardening information, household inventory, appraisals, and receipts for all home improvements and repairs.

- **FOOD:** Meeting the daily nutritional needs of your family. Topics include nutritional information, takeout and party menus, caterers, centerpiece inspirations, and recipes.

- **FAMILY AND FRIENDS:** Dealing with relational responsibilities as a parent and spouse, and with extended family, friends, and neighbors. Assign each family member a file folder color and store the following in each person's file: birth certificate, immunization records, report cards, résumés, hobby and sports information, prescriptions for eyeglasses and contacts, and pet records. If you have young children, the Missing Children Center in Tampa, Florida, recommends keeping a home identification file on each child to assist law enforcement officials in the event of abduction. The file should include a complete set of fingerprints as well as dental information.

- **FINANCES:** Managing the budget, bill paying, saving, investing, and charitable giving. Items to be filed in this department are banking records, spare checks, loan papers, insurance documents, receipts for purchases, mortgage or rental documents, and information regarding taxes, investments, retirement, and organizations to which you pay annual dues.

- **SPECIAL EVENTS:** Planning and coordinating occasions, celebrations, vacations, and family reunions that fall outside your normal routine. Documents to be filed here concern travel research, garage-sale records, birthday party and holiday ideas, and greeting card lists.

- TIME AND SCHEDULING: Managing the family calendar and daily schedule. Include here tips and articles on time management, last year's calendar, public transportation schedules, and children's school, sports, and activity calendars.

- PERSONAL: Caring for your body, nurturing your mind and spirit. This is where you will file information regarding your personal interests and hobbies, medical records, weight management, beauty and wardrobe information, and community and volunteer information.

–12–

RAKE LEAVES

KENT TAYLOR

Kent Taylor is the founder, director, and lead tour guide of the National Park Society. He is a park ranger in Colorado and author of the National Parks Lodging Guide.

The following tips won't eliminate the tedium of leaf raking altogether, but they will get you back in front of your new HDTV, snacks and cold drink in hand, in time for the second-half kickoff.

1. DECIDE IF YOU REALLY NEED TO PICK UP YOUR LEAVES. The answer is no if leaves have created only a thin covering over your lawn. However, keep in mind that if leaves cover too much lawn for too long, the grass beneath will weaken or die. Raking leaves, or mulching them, then becomes critical so that the leaves don't choke out the grass you worked so hard to cultivate all summer.

2. PRE-RAKE. Your first step is not to rake. As you mow during the early onset of fall you can bag many leaves, or mulch them if you have a mulching mower. Mulching will leave a visible layer of leaves that will enrich the soil as they decompose.

3. USE THE RIGHT TOOLS.

• **Leaf blowers** are best if you have an easy way to collect the leaves, such as putting them into a pickup truck for dumping elsewhere. Electric leaf blowers are quieter and more environmentally friendly, and work just as well as gas-powered models.

• **Vacuum leaf shredders** are great if you want to compost or bag the leaves and need to compress them into the smallest volume possible.

• **A proper rake** can significantly reduce the amount of time you spend raking. Use a standard-width twenty-four-inch rake equipped with a soft grip. Some unique products even offer specific ergonomic and efficiency advantages, which serve to reduce fatigue and quicken the task at hand: the Clog-Free Rake eliminates stuck leaves at the end of the rake; the Slapshot Rake uses the angle of the handle to allow you to clear three times as much ground as a traditional rake; the Ergo Rake features a contoured handle so it's easy on the back and requires no stooping or twisting.

• **Leaf scoops** are a fun item that may be just the thing to get the kids involved. These "hands" are designed to fit practically anyone, and enable you to pick up large bundles at a time.

• **Tarps** save energy and time by removing the need to rake leaves all the way across the lawn. Choose a medium-sized tarp, about 8 x 8 feet, with rope handles for easy hauling. A hefty material, whether canvas or heavyweight plastic, won't flap in the breeze and will resist tearing.

4. KNOW WHEN TO USE WHAT.

• Use leaf blower/vacs in vacuum mode to remove small amounts of leaves from tight spots where leaf rakes cannot reach.

- Use leaf blower/vacs in blower mode (in conjunction with tarps) to gather the bulk of your lawn's leaves into piles for removal by hand.

- Use leaf rakes for putting the finishing touches on lawn leaf removal or for leaf removal in small yards. Leaf rakes also help you to keep thatch (grass clippings and other undecomposed plant material) under control.

5. PREPARE. Dress in layers. Do a light warm-up before you pick up the rake. Maintain good posture and move your whole body rather than twisting to one side. Alternate raking on either side of your body. Drink water and take regular breaks.

6. RAKE AND BAG FASTER.

- **Rake in straight lines** so you know where you have been.

- **Work in small areas.** Rake up only what you can without changing position, and then bag the leaves you've collected. Then move to a new area and repeat. This is especially important if you have a bad back.

- **Learn the bagging trick.** Lay the bag down between your feet so that the opening is facing the pile. Use your heel to hold down one side of the bag and lift the other side with your hand. Pull the leaves into the bag with your free arm.

7. KNOW THE LAWS. Call your city or county manager to learn what rules apply when disposing of leaves. Check with your garbage collection service directly if it is not operated by the city or county.

8. MAINTAIN YOUR EQUIPMENT. Dry and clean your tools per manufacturer's recommendations and store safely, out of the weather.

–13–

COOK A MEAL

SAM ZIEN

Sam Zien, a.k.a. Sam the Cooking Guy, is the host of Just Cook This *on Discovery Health and the author of* Sam the Cooking Guy: Just a Bunch of Recipes.

1. KNOW WHAT YOU'RE MAKING. Too obvious? I think not. Remember the first time you rode a bike—you weren't very good, were you? It's the same when cooking something for the first time. If it's speed you're after, a tried-and-true recipe is the way to go— the Truffle-Roasted Peruvian Squab with Hand-Peeled Wild Inoki Mushrooms in a Saffron Buerre Blanc you've been dying to try is not.

2. USE FEWER INGREDIENTS. Let's make this simple: ten ingredients will normally take longer to put together and cook than five. So if you're searching through a cookbook, save the long recipes for when you're trying to impress the in-laws, not for when you're in need of a meal. Keep it simple and you can't go wrong.

3. HAVE YOUR INGREDIENTS AT THE READY. The French term for this is *mise en place* (pronounced "meez ahn plahs") and refers

to the practice of having everything in place. For a restaurant it means onions diced, herbs cut, garlic chopped—everything needed out and ready. At home it means the same thing. Remember that speed is of the essence, and having to stop to find your carrots, clean them, then cut and chop them will only waste valuable time—so prepare items in advance.

4. WHILE YOU'RE ON ONE STEP, THINK AHEAD TO THE NEXT. Ever watch a short-order cook work? When they get an order for a couple of fried eggs, hash browns, and whole wheat toast, they don't wait for the eggs to be done before putting in the toast or getting the hash browns on the griddle. They work on multiple steps at once. Cooking efficiently is like a symphony, with you playing all the instruments at the same time.

5. FASTER STARTS WITH FASTER—YA KNOW? A two-pound frozen chunk of meat is not going to get you and your hungry family eating anytime soon, so rethink it. Consider things you can keep on hand that'll let you go from nothing to eating in short order. Keep stocked any of the following and you'll be in good shape:

- Buy **frozen shrimp** and keep them in the freezer. To use, submerge in cool water for about fifteen minutes and they're ready. Throw a handful in a simmering soup, make some shrimp tacos, or stir-fry a bunch with some previously frozen veggies.

- And speaking of **veggies,** they're perfect sautéed in a sandwich with some melted cheese, stirred into an omelet, or even on pasta.

- And speaking of pasta, **pasta sauces** and **dried pasta** are genius for last-minute cooking. A simple pasta with garlic and olive oil can blow you away.

• Don't forget the **pizza crusts**—take one out of the freezer and turn on the oven. By the time you figure out what to put on it, it will be ready to go and so will the oven. Appetizer or main, it works for both.

6. CLEAN AS YOU GO. If you thought "quick" was only about the cooking, you were wrong, bucko. The whole speed thing depends on the *entire* process, and that means the cleaning-up part, too. So while the water is boiling, clean the counter. Or as something defrosts in the crow (the mi-CROW-wave), wash a spoon or two.

But enough theory already, how about we make something you can try your newly acquired quick skills on?

PESTO GRILLED SHRIMP

SERVES 6

Great as an appetizer or served with a salad. Plus, it has only two ingredients . . . well, technically three if you count the sticks. Use shrimp that are at least 31/40s. That just means there are between 31 and 40 shrimp per pound.

24 large shrimp, deveined, with shells and tails removed

24 wooden skewers

1 cup premade pesto (store-bought is easier)

1. Thread each shrimp on a skewer.
2. Coat the shrimp well with pesto and let sit about fifteen minutes. Reserve some pesto for serving.
3. Heat a grill or pan to medium-high.
4. Grill each skewered shrimp a couple of minutes on each side and serve with extra pesto for dipping.

–14–

CHOP VEGETABLES

MING TSAI

Ming Tsai is the host and executive producer of the public television cooking show Simply Ming. *He is the chef and owner of the world-renowned Blue Ginger restaurant in Wellesley, MA, and the author of* Blue Ginger, Simply Ming, *and* Ming's Master Recipes. *He has a line of Asian-inspired bamboo cutting boards and serveware with TruBamboo.*

hopping vegetables quickly, while still getting perfect, even cuts and keeping your hands cut-free, requires, first and foremost, solid knife skills.

KNIFE SKILLS

1. LEARN HOW TO HOLD A KNIFE. Grasp the end of the blade near the handle with your thumb and the side of your bent forefinger like you are making a fist and let the other three fingers curl naturally around the handle. Your forefinger should curl toward the handle, but the meat of

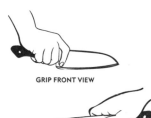

GRIP FRONT VIEW

GRIP REAR VIEW

the finger rests on the blade to steady the blade when cutting. This allows you to have control over the blade while taking advantage of the natural weight distribution of the knife.

2. BE AWARE OF YOUR OTHER HAND. You should hold the vegetable with your other hand formed into a claw, fingers bent back toward you on top of the vegetable, so that your knuckles come into contact with the flat side of the blade. Use your pinkie and thumb to help anchor each side of the item and keep it in place. This keeps your fingertips out of the way of the cutting surface of the blade.

3. MASTER THE ROCKING MOTION. This is how you will chop quickly and precisely. Keep the tip of the knife on the cutting board and rock the blade backward and forward, using a fluid, continual motion. Practice this on the board itself. When you're comfortable enough to graduate to an actual vegetable, use the method described in step 2. You can either push or pull the knife blade as you cut, depending on what you're cutting and your preferred technique. If you're slicing a tomato, for instance, you can't usually just bring the blade down on the tomato—you'll squish it. You either need to start with the tip of the blade pointed toward the board and slice down with the front portion of the blade and away as you bring the end of the blade through the tomato, pushing the knife away from you, or you can start with the end of the blade at the tomato, bring it down, and follow through with the rest of the blade, pulling the knife toward you as you slice.

Pair your knife skills with these prep pointers for faster chopping:

USE A GOOD, SHARP KNIFE

A sharp knife is your best tool for efficient kitchen work. I like to use a cleaver for most chopping jobs because it has a big blade with some weight behind it, so it goes through large, firm veggies like eggplant easily and I can use the wide surface of the blade to scoop up the chopped product and take it directly to the pot—a great time-saver.

GET A BAMBOO BOARD

I love bamboo because it is extremely durable—stronger than wood—yet doesn't harm the knife's edge. It's also one of the most renewable resources in the world, so it's eco-friendly. Never use glass or cut on granite or marble, which will quickly dull your knife and make chopping a chore and potentially hazardous.

GET YOUR MISE TOGETHER

In the culinary world, we use the term *mise en place*, which means, roughly, having everything in its place. If you know you need to chop onions, tomatoes, and zucchini, make sure your tomatoes and zucchini are washed and your onions are peeled and they're all at your fingertips, with small containers ready to receive the chopped product. I would chop the zucchini first, then the onions, then the tomatoes. Why in that order? Zucchini is dry and easy to clean up; onions are dry, but cutting them can leave behind small pieces of their layers, so you'll need to give the board a quick wipe before you can move on; and tomatoes are very juicy and will get the board the dirtiest.

Now that you've mastered the basics of prepared chopping, you can focus on fine-tuning and shaving a few more minutes off your active chopping time.

SPECIALTY SKILLS

Besides the basic rocking motion, there are a few specialty cuts and uses for your knife that speed things up.

TO BREAK DOWN AN ONION, TOMATO, OR OTHER ROUNDED VEGGIE:

First, cut it in half, then put one of the halves cut side down and make a series of lengthwise cuts, taking care to leave about one-eighth to one-quarter of an inch intact and uncut at one end. This holds the veggie together for the next step. Now cut the veggie across the center in the other direction (parallel to the board), again taking care to leave the last bit intact and uncut. Now you can slice across the top, producing evenly chopped pieces and cutting your time in half.

TO BREAK DOWN GARLIC:

Using the flat side of the blade, place it as flat as possible on the garlic and smack the heel of your palm onto the blade (make sure the cutting edge is angled down so you don't bring your hand down on it). This breaks down the garlic and lessens chopping time.

With these few small changes to your prep routine you can arrive more quickly at the best part—eating!

–15–

WASH DISHES

PETE JORDAN

Pete Jordan is the author of Dishwasher: One Man's
Quest to Wash Dishes in All Fifty States.

Nobody likes to wash dishes—not even me. When dishing on
dishes, I'm all business. Here's what you need to know:

1. SKIP THE MACHINE. I've never taken it easy on myself by
using a home dishwasher. Judging from the dishes I've had to eat
off in homes that do employ machines, I can attest only that they're
far too wimpy for the task, unlike restaurants' industrial-strength
dish machines, which blast dishes to a sparkling clean. So, at
home, it's always a sinkful of sudsy water for me.

2. NO GLOVES. Seeing whether a dish is clean is one thing, but
feeling whether it's clean is just as important. With gloves, it's
impossible to feel the residue crud on plates. Wearing gloves while
dishwashing is like wearing a raincoat while showering.

3. LIMIT DISH USE. The best way to make dishwashing easier
is to simply limit the amount of dishes that need to be washed.
Henry David Thoreau—a dude who apparently hated unnecesary
dishwashing—advocated in *Walden:* "Simplify, simplify. Instead
of three meals a day, if it be necessary eat but one; instead of

a hundred dishes, five; and reduce other things in proportion. . . ."

Use the side of the fork to cut that chicken breast on your plate and leave the knife clean and unused in the drawer. Eat meals directly out of the pots and pans they're cooked in and give the plates and bowls a night off. And always drink right out of the carton. (Just this morning, my wife drank orange juice out of the carton. "You see?" she said, seeking my approval. I saw, and indeed I beamed with pride—just as Thoreau would have done.)

4. THE SOAK. Whether you're a professional busting suds eight to twelve hours a day or an amateur doing the deed at home, a good prolonged soaking will always be appreciated. Let the water do the work for you. More soaking equals less scrubbing. Plus, it buys you time. After a big meal, the household's dishwasher may not feel like prying him or herself off the couch to go tackle the dishes. What to do? Fill a pot with hot soapy water and toss all the silverware in it. Fill any other dirty cookware with hot soapy water. Then return to the couch and announce to the household's cook, "The dishes really need to soak overnight." (This is usually acceptable behavior in my household.)

5. ROUTINE. This is important in terms of both when to wash dishes and in what order. What works best for me is to wash dishes at the same time every day. Lately, this has been at eight AM while my son sits beside me eating breakfast and I'm listening to the radio.

Washing items in order from cleanest to filthiest makes the hot, soapy water last longer. First, cups and glasses are washed and set aside. Then silverware. Then bowls and plates. Finally, the pots and pans. Then all is rinsed under warm running water (as hot as you can bear) and set in a drying rack. After everything is towel-dried and put away, enjoy the sight of the clean kitchen before it's once again polluted with dirty dishes.

-16-

FIND A LOST OBJECT

MICHAEL SOLOMON

Michael Solomon is a findologist and the author of
How to Find Lost Objects.

Nothing is more distressing than having misplaced some vital possession—a set of keys, a wallet, an important document. Yet lost objects *can* be found, quickly and easily. How? By applying my twelve principles. Here they are:

1. DON'T LOOK FOR IT. That is to say, don't look for it yet. Wait until you are in the proper frame of mind, and are prepared to search *systematically*.

2. IT'S NOT LOST—YOU ARE. Accept that the problem is not with the object—it's with you! For there are no lost objects—only unsystematic searchers.

3. REMEMBER THE THREE C'S. Your essential tools for getting in the right frame of mind:

Comfort. Sit down and relax. Settle back and breathe deeply.

Calmness. Now let that distress and agitation dissolve away.

Sure, you're upset with yourself for having lost a vital possession. But calm down and empty your mind of all unsettling thoughts.

Confidence. Tell yourself that it's going to be quick and easy—that missing object hasn't got a chance!

Okay, now you're ready to hunt down that missing object.

4. IT'S WHERE IT'S SUPPOSED TO BE. Amazingly, our possessions are often right where they're supposed to be. Can't locate your raincoat? Check the closet where it's supposed to be kept (Someone may have hung it up for you.)

5. DOMESTIC DRIFT. Sadly, things seldom get put back where they belong. So check the place where the missing object was last used. You may be pleasantly surprised.

6. YOU'RE LOOKING RIGHT AT IT. Curiously, it is possible to look directly at a lost object and not see it. We've become so agitated that we don't perceive what is right in front of us. So calm down (remember the Three Cs?). You may find yourself staring right at those elusive keys.

7. THE CAMOUFLAGE EFFECT. Your object may be right where you recall having had it, or where it's usually kept, but it has become covered up. Check beneath anything that might have been inadvertently placed on top of the object and be hiding it from view. (Newspapers and sombreros are among the most common offenders.)

8. THINK BACK. Can't find your glasses? Somewhere in your unconscious mind, you *know* their location because you left them there! Think back, retrieve the memory, and make a beeline for those glasses.

9. THE EUREKA ZONE. Many objects are in the immediate vicinity of where you thought they were—they've merely undergone a

displacement. (A pair of scissors, for example, has been shoved to the rear of its drawer.) Objects tend to travel no more than eighteen inches from their original location. So measure a radius of eighteen inches—that's your Eureka Zone. Now search it *meticulously.*

10. LOOK ONCE, LOOK WELL. Don't keep going back to check a particular site, no matter how promising. If it wasn't there the first time, it won't be there the second. (Assuming, of course, that your initial check was meticulous.)

11. TAIL THYSELF. Simply follow your own trail. Physically retrace your steps from the last place you remember having the object, and, like a detective, you may cry out, "Aha!"

12. IT WASN'T YOU. Occasionally, an object hasn't been misplaced—it's been misappropriated. Approach the likely culprit and ask (as tactfully as possible) if he has perhaps taken your magazine or borrowed your umbrella.

By now you should have located your object—and usually within minutes!

WORK

–17–

FIND YOUR CALLING

RICHARD BOLLES

Richard Bolles is the author of What Color Is Your Parachute?: A Practical Manual For Job-Hunters and Career Changers. *Revised annually, it is the most popular career guide in the world, with 10 million copies in print.*

I f we are to understand the subject of our *calling*, we need to discuss our personal histories and how we have made decisions about our callings in life. There are deep lessons we can learn from one another. Here is my own story:

When I was fourteen, I felt my calling in life was to be a *newspaperman.* I loved my dad, and he was a newspaperman. So I felt I had the same calling.

By the time I was nineteen, I had grown up. I now felt my calling was to be a *chemical engineer.* This, because I loved magic and felt there was magic in the way that chemical elements combined to produce a new thing. So I enrolled in a scientific university.

Halfway through college, when I was twenty-one, I felt called to be a *minister* of the Christian gospel. This, because I loved Jesus and was heart struck when I discovered that many churches were closing for lack of a minister. So I transferred to a liberal arts college and after graduation entered a seminary and was ordained.

That lasted until I was forty-two, when I felt a new calling: to be a *vocational writer and counselor.* This, because after writing sermons for many years I found that people in my care who were out of work needed special help, and I loved using my writing and researching skills to assist them.

When I reached my fifties I felt an additional calling, so I ended up with two: not only was I a writer but now I wanted also to be a *wise man.* I loved wisdom: teaching people to distinguish what mattered more from what mattered less, and the ability to see things in a larger context, like the universe, or God.

Now, what can you learn from such a history as mine?

First, your calling, or "vocation," is not necessarily one fixed, immutable calling from birth to death. For some people, there may just be one, like the ninety-one-year-old actress who reflects: "I always knew I wanted to be an actress." But your life may instead be a series of callings, each one (or even two callings at the same time) true and correct for that period of your life, depending on which of your unique gifts you most love to use and what problems in the world grip your attention. Either or both of those may change during your lifetime. And with that, so does your calling.

Second, it may take quite some time to discover what your calling is. It is not necessarily a task that can be rushed. Herminia Ibarra, a professor at *Insead* in France, found, in a study of thirty-nine people with advanced degrees, that making a move to a new career or calling typically took her subjects about four years. If you do not hold an advanced degree it may take less time—typically two years—as I found in a long-term study of my own students in two-week workshops from 1974 to 2000.

Third, there are ways to speed up the discerning of your true calling (or callings). How? You can look around at all the people you know, or have heard of, and decide which ones you admire most. Then you can study what they are doing with their lives, and see if you feel called to pursue something similar.

You can look around at the world and decide which particular problem you want to work on or help solve, and then look inward to see which of the talents and gifts you have been given you most want to use in dealing with that problem.

Calling, after all, is rooted in the language of faith, though those roots are often forgotten. *Calling* implies one who calls. *Vocation* is the same word, in more ancient language (Latin). The impulse to discern our calling was, from the start, a religious impulse.

And the deepest question when reflecting on that impulse ends up being not "*What* do you feel called to do?" but "*Whom* do you feel called to be?"

–18–

FIND AND LAND A JOB

ROB McGOVERN

Rob McGovern is the author of Bring Your "A" Game: The Top 10 Career Secrets of the High Achiever. *He is the CEO of Jobfox, a career site that uses precision matching technology and enables professionals to create Web pages to showcase their skills and talents. McGovern is also the original founder of CareerBuilder.com.*

To find and land your dream job quickly, you need to stand out in a crowd. Here's how:

• KNOW YOURSELF. Develop a self-directed career plan. Companies want people who demonstrate an upward trajectory of personal and professional growth. With a self-directed career plan in place, it will be easy to express how you got to where you are today and where you are going with your next job. Do this right, and you will find you are a rare and valued commodity. Ignore it and you will find your résumé in the recruiter's trash bin and job interviews will be difficult. Recruiters immediately look for job experience inconsistencies. It's a quick way for them to weed out pretenders from experienced contenders.

- MARKET YOURSELF. Personal branding has never been more important. In addition to the résumé and cover letter, the new tools of the successful job hunt include personal Web pages, blogs, online portfolios, and smart social networking practices. In today's world, if you can't be "Googled," you don't exist. When used professionally, Internet tools also help demonstrate intangibles such as work and life passions, writing abilities, creativity, and interpersonal skills.

- USE CAUTION ONLINE. Unfortunately, as many younger MySpace and other social networking users have learned, the way you use Internet tools can backfire. There are many documented cases of companies that have eliminated qualified candidates from consideration after viewing unsavory content on a personal Web page or social networking site.

- FACE-TO-FACE NETWORKING. Tell everyone you are looking. Join trade associations and attend professional group functions on a regular basis. Keep in mind that there are thousands of new jobs created that are never posted publicly. These positions are often filled through informal networking channels.

- SEARCH ONLINE. Job boards and niche job sites provide scores of opportunities. Also, don't forget to check specific company sites for job listings. Update your résumé frequently on these boards. New and refreshed résumés are brought to the top of the pile for recruiter consideration. For the same reason, check the sites often for new job listings.

- KNOW THE BUZZWORDS. Recruiters often use keyword searches of résumés to get to the candidates with the general skills they're looking for. Be sure to include the right skill words and industry terms in your résumé and when completing online application forms. Look at current job postings to get an idea of the keywords companies search for.

- CONNECT YOURSELF. Got voice mail, e-mail, and instant messaging? IM, especially, is emerging as a favorite of recruiters who want to be able to reach candidates when they are available online. Get yourself an IM account.

- BE READY FROM THE START. Most recruiters screen a short list of candidates with a brief telephone interview. With a thought-out career plan, be ready—at a moment's notice—to explain your career path strategy and how the job under discussion is a perfect fit based on your past skills, accomplishments, and vision for the future.

- REHEARSE YOUR SUCCESSES. While most job seekers can talk about their skills, most aren't prepared with real examples of how their skills helped move an organization forward. What actions led to what results? Remember, the recruiter has already whittled down the candidate list to only those with the prerequisite skills. To stand out, use stories of past accomplishments to demonstrate your skills in action.

- FOLLOW UP. After every interaction with the organization, send a well-crafted e-mail expressing your appreciation and excitement about the opportunity. If you don't hear back from the organization after a few days, contact the recruiter or hiring manager to inquire about next steps.

-19-

WAKE UP

ZAC UNGER

Zac Unger is a firefighter in Oakland, California.

He is the author of Working Fire:

The Making of an Accidental Fireman.

Despite what you may have been led to believe, there is no such thing as "half-awake" or "half-asleep." You're either awake or you're asleep, end of discussion. If you can recognize this simple fact, then you're 90 percent of the way to waking up quickly

The reason you have trouble waking up is because you feel as though you *deserve* more sleep. You don't. There's nothing in the Constitution about lounging around in bed, and the snooze button is not your birthright. In my line of work an alarm is an alarm; it rings and I get up no matter how much sleep I've had so far that night. You need to do the same thing. No more bemoaning your sleepy fate. Maybe you got only four hours of sleep last night, but that's a problem you need to deal with on the nighttime end of things, not in the morning.

Here are some concrete strategies to make it feel less like boot camp and more like tough love:

WAKE UP YOUR MIND

When you're tired it's easy to be mentally lazy, to nurse a glass of orange juice and allow yourself to go numb for thirty minutes. But the truth is that if you can afford thirty minutes of AM stupidity, then you probably could have afforded another half hour of sleep. As soon as that alarm rings, put yourself though some quick mental gymnastics. Count to one thousand by seventeens. Try to remember the exact wording and placement of yesterday's newspaper headlines. Spell your street name backward. The specifics don't matter—just do something different, new, and mentally challenging. It will get your brain churning and, more important, distract you from the self-pity you feel at being awake.

WAKE UP YOUR BODY

The physical specimen you wake up with is the same one that you put to bed last night, so don't cut it any slack just because the light is different. Your muscles are just as strong, your bones are the same size, and you didn't get *that* much older and more infirm overnight. Get your body doing something immediately in order to escape the early morning doldrums. This isn't hard; we're not talking sumo wrestling here. Put away the dishes, take out the garbage, water the plants. It doesn't really matter what you do; just get your body working in order to reinforce the fact that you and your bed have just gotten a quickie divorce.

AVOID CRUTCHES

All of those things that you think of as your "morning routine" are ruses you concoct to pretend that you're still asleep. The couch is just an extension of the bed, the shower is just another dream, and the time you spend staring at the glowing coils of the toaster is a few minutes that you'll never get back. You don't need anything external in order to wake up. Coffee is counterfeit alertness, morning sun salutations are ridiculous; you already have everything you need in order to wake up fast.

The best part about learning to wake up quickly is that you no longer need to waste all that time in the morning moping around the house. You can use that time for whatever you want, but I suggest using it for sleep. If you get nine hours of sleep, then learning how to wake up quickly is like a ten-foot-tall man figuring out how to dunk a basketball.

So use the tricks above, but more than anything else, when the alarm rings, that's it—your night is over. Feet on the floor, ass in your pants, bagel in your face, and out the door you go.

–20–

GET READY IN THE MORNING

HANNAH STORM

Hannah Storm is the morning coanchor of ESPN's
SportsCenter. *She was the coanchor of* The Early Show
on CBS for more than five years.

After more than five years of getting up before the crack of dawn, I think I have this getting-ready-fast thing down pat. The golden rule is be organized!

Mornings can quickly become overwhelming if you don't have a well-designed and well-executed plan. Whether you have kids running around, a spouse slowing you down, or simply feel too scatterbrained or overwhelmed to get ready efficiently, streamlining your morning routine is the answer to your woes. Believe me, when you're waking at four AM and have dozens of daily responsibilities to juggle, you need to be prepared or you'll never make it out of the house on time. So here are my top tips for getting you ready and on your way:

- Make your day as structured as possible. One of the first things I did after taking the *Early Show* job was to create a simple chart, with each hour of the day listed on the left and corresponding blank spaces on the right. Each night before I went to bed I filled out one of these charts for the following day. In the blank spaces I wrote information about where my three kids were going on an hourly basis, what needed to be taken to school, and errands and tasks that needed to be completed. I set that piece of paper on the kitchen counter each morning for everyone to look at and follow throughout the day so that my whole family was literally on the same page. It was an invaluable guide for the entire household. More important, with my day mapped out, I could fly out of bed in the morning with purpose!

- Take care of things the night before. Make sure kids' homework and bags are packed, anything special they'll need for school is pulled, and their clothing is ready to go. There's nothing worse than scrambling for matching mittens in the morning!

- Have a wardrobe plan. As you know, something unexpected always comes up in the morning, so the last thing you want to stress about is what you're going to wear. Check out the weather report the previous night and pull out your own clothes in advance. If you plan on working out, have your gym bag and toiletries ready to go.

- Keep your bathroom and makeup station clutter-free. Put the basics within easy reach. Things like your moisturizer, toothpaste, deodorant, and makeup should always be in the same place so you know right where to access them in the morning.

- Set your coffeemaker to brew automatically a few minutes before you wake up; not only will you have your cup of coffee ready to go but the great aroma will help you wake up.

- Oversleeping is the surest way to slow yourself down. So set TWO alarm clocks if you need to get up at a certain time—one electric and one battery-operated—just in case.

As for the weekends, all bets are off! Relax and enjoy.

–21–

ACHIEVE SUCCESS

RICHARD ST. JOHN

> *Richard St. John is a success analyst and author who spent ten years interviewing more than five hundred successful people. His books are* 8 to Be Great *and* Stupid, Ugly, Unlucky and Rich.

There is no such thing as overnight success—it takes time to succeed at anything. But that doesn't mean you can't speed up the process. With that in mind, here are five tips to help you achieve success faster:

1. FUEL UP WITH PASSION

If you want to travel faster on the road to success you'll need to fuel up. Just any old fuel won't do—you're going to need super-high-octane fuel. And that fuel is passion. Loving what you do is the instant energizer that makes you enthusiastic, gets you working harder and moving faster, and gives you the stamina to persist. As neurosurgeon Keith Black says, "Energy comes from within if you love what you do." So find something you love and get super-charged with passion.

2. STAY FOCUSED

Advertising guru Jay Chiat told me, "The single universal quality among every successful person I know is they all have an incredibly high level of energy focused on one thing." Focus is critical to achieving success at anything. If you're all over the map it will take longer to reach your destination. And the faster you want to get there, the more you need to focus, just as driving down a narrow road at 60 mph requires more focus than at 30 mph. It's not a drag race in which you need to stay focused for only a few seconds. It's more like the Indy 500, which requires intense sustained focus for hundreds of miles.

3. ELIMINATE DISTRACTIONS

Distractions are the enemy of focused attention. A successful race car driver said to me, "A little bit of distraction on the racetrack and you could have a really bad day." The same applies on the fast track to success. Entertainment, cell phones, video games, Web surfing, parties—they all defocus you and cause crashes and delays on the road to success. That's why successful people eliminate distractions. Renowned venture capitalist Steve Jurvetson says, "You can't do it all, so I cut out a lot of extraneous things. I haven't watched television for eighteen years. I don't miss it." Deborah McGuinness, senior research scientist at Stanford, said to me, "Getting my degree, every year I cut out things. I remember the year I sacrificed movies. I just said, 'I can't afford the time. I'll put movies back in my life again once I finish the Ph.D.'" What distractions are *you* willing to eliminate today in order to achieve faster success tomorrow?

4. DON'T LOOK BACK

Successful people don't look back. Toronto's City TV president Moses Znaimer said to me, "I don't have much of a going back memory. I don't remember bad things. I'm very future-oriented." The famous architect Frank Lloyd Wright even had the rear window of his car covered because, he said, "I never look behind." If you want to achieve success faster you'll need to keep your eyes on the road ahead. We all take wrong turns, make mistakes, and fail. But stopping to look back eats up valuable time that could be used to move forward. So when you fail, spend five minutes feeling sorry for yourself, then get up and keep moving toward success. It's better to have an imagination that looks ahead than a memory that looks back.

5. BE IMPATIENT

Patience is often seen as a virtue, but many successful people got to where they are by having absolutely no patience. Nobel Prize winner James Watson, the codiscoverer of DNA structure, said to me, "I'm very impatient, and rather intolerant of people who aren't impatient when something needs to be done. I like to move fast." Speed is important, and that's why so many successful people are always in a hurry. Henry Kravis said he's been in a hurry all his life. Henry hurried all the way to the top as cofounder of KKR, the world's biggest buyout firm. If you want to reach success quickly, be impatient and in a hurry to succeed.

There you have it—five tips to achieve success faster. Now stop listening to me and get out there and do something.

–22–

REDUCE THE LENGTH OF MEETINGS

VERNE HARNISH

Verne Harnish is the CEO of Gazelles, an executive leadership training company, and the founder of Entrepreneurs' Organization (EO). He writes the syndicated column "The Growth Guy" and is the author of Mastering the Rockefeller Habits. Fortune Small Business *magazine named Harnish one of the Top 10 Minds in Small Business.*

You can save an hour or more each day and shorten your meetings by implementing just one effective tool—a fifteen-minute daily huddle with your team.

This recommendation is often met with cries of "We're too busy!" or "We don't need a huddle when we're seeing one another all day long." But before dismissing the idea, consider that an effective daily meeting rhythm is at the heart of management practices used by many esteemed groups, from the top teams at

Ritz-Carlton to the assembly floors of Dell to the Oval Office of the White House.

Teams that huddle daily find they interrupt one another considerably less, whether via e-mail or "drive-bys," as people wait to address issues until the huddle. Meeting daily also clears up issues that otherwise linger, allowing weekly meetings to be shorter and more focused and preventing issues of immediate concern from growing bigger.

Make your daily huddle effective by following these guidelines:

1. Start at a specific time each day, and make it an odd one, like 8:08 AM or 4:44 PM. I've observed a strange psychological pattern: people are more likely to be prompt when the start time is not on the half or quarter hour. (Worried that you'll forget the meeting while traveling? Set a recurring reminder alarm on your cell phone or BlackBerry.)

2. Start the meeting on time whether everyone is present or not—this will signal that you don't wait for stragglers. I've been in the middle of intense meetings with clients and venture capitalists and still told them that I needed to break for my daily meeting. Doing so will gain you respect—a disciplined person exudes success.

3. Make attendance and on-time arrival mandatory, and accept no excuses.

4. If you want to keep the meeting very short, have everyone stand up for its entirety.

5. End the meeting on time. The best way to do this is to back one meeting up against another regular meeting or appointment.

The Agenda: It should be the same every day, with just three five-minute segments:

1. WHAT'S UP?

In the first five minutes, each attendee shares what will be going on in the next twenty-four hours. This makes people aware of potential conflicts, crossed agendas, and missed opportunities. The key is to highlight specifics rather than simply reading to-do lists. For example, "I'm meeting with John Smith at ABC firm to discuss our buyback policy," rather than, "I have some customer meetings today." Someone might know something about John Smith; a colleague might question why you're seeing John Smith versus Mary Jones; or another might feel he should be in the meeting.

2. DAILY METRICS/KEY PERFORMANCE INDICATORS (KPIs)

Next, review whatever daily measurements your company uses to track progress, highlighting any unusual trends. There's something useful about hearing the information even when it's also available via spreadsheet—hearing is a powerful sense that reinforces memory. What you're trying to discern are the patterns and trends of the business. By reviewing key data daily, you won't need to spend as much time on it at the weekly and monthly meetings.

3. WHERE ARE YOU STUCK?

This is the most important agenda item. You're looking for bottlenecks. People verbalizing (for the whole group to hear) their fears, struggles, and concerns is the first step to solving problems, because "until the mouth runs, the brain won't engage." Keep in mind that the only people who aren't getting stuck on occasion are either lying or not doing anything. Important as it is, however, the bottleneck conversation shouldn't be allowed to drift into problem solving. It's okay if somebody wants to reply to a bottleneck by saying "Call so-and-so," but if two people start engaging over an issue, politely suggest they "take it off-line." Remember: The daily meeting needs to be kept short. It's for problem identification, not problem solving.

While reading *Titan,* the biography of John D. Rockefeller, I was struck by the fact that Rockefeller had lunch with his top team every day. He insisted that this routine was crucial in the success and global reach of his company—and it will be for your firm as well.

–23–

MAKE YOUR COMPUTER RUN FASTER

ROBERT STEPHENS

Robert Stephens is the founder of The Geek Squad, the largest tech support company in the United States, with more than seventeen thousand agents. He is the author of The Geek Squad Guide to Solving Any Computer Glitch.

L et's get one thing straight: it's not your fault. Every time computer technicians show up to make a house call, you start apologizing for being dumb about technology. That's just not true. It's the technology that's dumb and too hard to use. Also, please don't be overly impressed by the technical ability of computer geeks—we know this much only because we have each sacrificed more than one thousand Saturday nights to learn all this stuff.

Let's start with the basics:

BACK UP EVERYTHING ON A FLASH DRIVE
AND EXTERNAL HARD DRIVE

While most of the advice below should be safe enough for a novice to follow, the speed of your computer does not matter if you have lost your files. I know, I know, you've been promising to back up everything for quite some time now. If you always have those important documents on a flash drive, you'll be able to access them from just about anywhere. I prefer the kind that actually clips onto your keychain so you don't have to think about where you left it.

ADD RAM

Just about every task that your computer performs passes through small chips called "RAM," or, more plainly, "memory." It's like this: you can remember more stuff if you have more paper to write things down on. It's the same with your computer. It can do more if it has more memory. So take it to your nearest computer shop and ask them to "max the RAM"—meaning add as much RAM as the computer can handle.

USE IT OR LOSE IT

Both Macintosh and Windows allow you to add or remove applications. In Windows, "Add or Remove Programs" is a feature located in your Control Panel. If you don't recognize the items listed here, go for it and remove those. Note: If you are more adventurous, use *msconfig* in Windows (click Run and type "msconfig") and uncheck items in the Startup tab. You can always turn some items back on if you need to.

DEFRAG BY USING DISK CLEANUP WIZARD

Your hard drive is similar to your garage. Over time, unseen clutter emerges through day-to-day use. Files and pieces of files are kept all over the place on your hard drive, meaning untidiness that can cause subtle slowdowns in your computer's speed. This Windows-based utility can automate a few smaller tasks to clean up your computer. You'll find the Disk Cleanup Wizard located in the "Accessories" section of your Start menu under "System Tools." Mac OSX users rejoice—your Mac does this for you.

Here are a couple of less common but equally effective methods to make things faster:

SWITCH TO WEB-BASED APPLICATIONS

More and more applications run over the Web, and this offers some distinct advantages over regular, installed software. Instead of taking up disk space and valuable system resources, you simply access these programs via your Web browser. In addition to Web-based e-mail, you can also now create documents, spreadsheets, and even slideshow presentations online. An added advantage is that no backups are required, as your work is saved on the Web. Caveat: Stick with a long-term brand name like Google and try their new Google Apps (think a Web version of Microsoft Office).

TRY A NEW WEB BROWSER

With more and more of your work moving online, a Web browser can sometimes help speed things up. Firefox (www.firefox.com) is a free, open-source browser that often makes working online faster.

There are some riskier, more advanced techniques that you can perform to boost the speed of your computer until you purchase your next whole system upgrade. However, these are better left to professionals, and you are best advised to call one rather than attempt them yourself. Just remember to create a' full system backup first.

–24–

RETURN PHONE CALLS

MICHAEL SHVO

Michael Shvo is the president of SHVO, a luxury real estate marketing firm based in New York. SHVO is the driving force behind some of the world's most celebrated new-development residences in the United States, Asia, the Middle East, and Central America. He receives an average of 180 phone calls per day.

R eturning phone calls is an art form. When and how you call someone back is not only a reflection on you, but also indicates your work ethic and approach to both business and personal relationships. My method is similar to the messages my executive assistant and I leave for others: simple and direct. Doing business in every time zone on a daily basis demands that I return calls as quickly as possible. This is my strategy:

1. MAKE PHONE TIME

If you're super time-crunched, like me, carve out time during the day to devote specifically to calls—no e-mails, no meetings, no interruptions. You'll be surprised by how many names get crossed off your list when you focus exclusively on the task at hand.

2. PRIORITIZE

Whether personal or business, all calls are equally important and deserve your time and attention—some are just more time-sensitive than others. So return the most urgent calls first.

3. TRAVEL TIME

My most productive time for catching up on calls is when I'm sitting in my car. Being in transit is precious phone time, whether you're driving or on the train (just be mindful of your etiquette when making calls while taking public transportation).

4. PLAY PHONE TAG

When returning calls it's inevitable that you'll get caught up in some frustrating games of phone tag. People are busy, and there's a good chance the person you're trying to reach is unavailable. But if you have to get in touch, you're going to have to play the game—so be persistent.

5. KEEP IT BRIEF

If you reach a person's voice mail or someone else who is going to pass a message on to its intended recipient, leave just a brief message stating your name and contact information. People have neither the time nor the attention span to listen to long messages, and being succinct on a consistent basis will save you precious minutes.

6. STAY DETERMINED

Stay away from message dumping (e.g., calling a person's office to leave a message at 9 PM when you know they've left for the day). This practice is transparent and reflects poorly on you. The only way to close a deal or reach a resolution on something is to speak with the person directly.

7. ACKNOWLEDGE A MESSAGE

If you're unable to return a call on time, send a quick e-mail or have someone contact the person on your behalf to acknowledge that you received the message. It's important that the caller doesn't feel neglected. It might take you a day or two to get back to him, but recognizing his message in the meantime makes all the difference.

8. DON'T WATCH THE CLOCK

Never set a time limit on a call before the conversation starts; you can't put a time frame on closing a deal.

9. CUT IT SHORT

Though you don't want to cut a productive conversation off early, when you're pressed for time and dealing with a talkative person, it's essential to move on. Simply tell the person that you have to attend to another obligation—step into a meeting or call someone back. It's the simplest, most direct approach, and people will respect and appreciate your frankness.

10. RETURN MORE CALLS

The number of calls I return each day is the same number that I receive plus several more (from previous days). Make it a habit to return more calls than you get that day and you'll train yourself to fly through your messages efficiently.

–25–

WADE THROUGH INFORMATION

SAMANTHA WEEKS

Major Samantha Weeks is the first female solo pilot for the Thunderbirds, the elite Air Demonstration Squadron of the United States Air Force.

Imagine being strapped into the cockpit of an F-16 fighter jet, soaring around trees, hills, and clouds while flying just 150 feet off the ground at more than 500 mph. A glance forward reveals a matching F-16 flying dead ahead closing in at nearly 1000 mph. With mere split seconds separating a purposeful, breathtaking maneuver from an unexpected collision, what makes the difference? Situational awareness.

Situational awareness (or, in preferred slang, SA) is an expression widely used in the military—especially the fighter pilot community. It refers to the mental digestion of information—the evaluation and appreciation of events, interactions, objects, environmental conditions, and other situation-specific factors affecting human performance in complex and dynamic tasks. Simply put, SA is the mental filter that helps a good pilot decide which inputs are critical now, and which can be addressed five seconds from now.

In other words, situational awareness is common sense intensified. Constant training in the air enhanced my professional life on the ground. I can wade through information in a quick, expeditious fashion and make a decision promptly but accurately And you can, too.

A fighter pilot learns how to fly, fight, and win through a building-block approach. This approach allows you to build your experiences, enhance your own natural abilities, and train your mind through daily exercises. To build your SA bubble, and thereby increase your ability to absorb information, process it faster, and take the appropriate action, follow these steps:

1. USE THE BUILDING-BLOCK APPROACH

To build a useful SA bubble, start with what you already know by accepting the facts as they are. Next, expand your bubble by factoring in your knowledge of any variables. This building-block approach will allow you to succeed in any endeavor by increasing your situational awareness.

Don't try to fly an F-16 on day one; don't try to beat Jeff Gordon on the track when you first get your driver's license. Start with the basics and work to build your abilities. Add more to your plate only after you've come close to mastering one activity. Take careful steps to absorb new information at the proper pace. If too much is added too fast, you will experience costly setbacks.

2. VISUALIZE

Imagine the perfect situation and visualize every aspect of your day/project/maneuvers from start to finish. This enables your brain to recall it from long-term memory so you have something to fall back on when the time arrives for action. Visualization provides more practice, repetition, and experience.

3. BUILD GOOD PATTERNS

To maximize short- and long-term memory and make the most of visualization, build good habit patterns. This enables you to absorb incoming information more quickly because you won't have to spend brain bytes deciding where to look for proper guidance.

4. PRACTICE

Train like you fight. Practice like you play. Make every minute count. Every educational experience should be as realistic as possible so that you build the most accurate experience database, thus increasing your SA bubble and maximizing your abilities, experience, and understanding.

5. EVALUATE

Fighter pilots fly a mission for an average of thirty minutes, yet the debrief evaluation of that flight will take two to four hours. Lessons learned in debrief contribute to a bigger SA bubble and allow you to perform better the next day. Apply this principle by creating your own debrief; find a person or team who will talk you through and assess your experiences for future improvements.

6. NEVER GET COMPLACENT

It's imperative to stay mentally engaged, even if you are in a situation or circumstance you experience repeatedly. Accomplish this by being goal-oriented. SA is largely influenced by your goals and expectations. Try to be better every day and that desire will keep you mentally alert and your SA at its peak.

Anyone can apply these principles to his or her daily routine. SA is really just about processing information quickly and accurately by learning from your past experiences, maximizing your own innate potential, and training in the same manner in which you want to perform. With a larger SA bubble, you'll feel more grounded in the environment and process all that is around you faster and better.

–26–

LEARN NAMES

JERRY LUCAS

Jerry Lucas, a.k.a. Doctor Memory, is a former pro basketball player turned memory expert and educator. He was named one of the NBA's 50 Greatest Basketball Players in NBA History and is a member of the Basketball Hall of Fame. Lucas has authored and coauthored more than sixty books, including The Memory Book, *which has sold more than 2 million copies.*

How many times have you found yourself saying, "I remember your face, but I'm sorry, I just can't seem to remember your name"? I bet you've never said something like this, though: "Hi, Mary. You know, I remember your name, but I just can't seem to remember your face." Why do you remember faces and not names? Because you *see* the face but only *hear* the name. Our minds register pictures of tangible objects automatically and, more important, re-create them by just thinking of them. Let me prove it to you by asking you *not* to do something.

Please do *not* see a zebra in your mind. That's right; do not see a zebra! Saw a zebra, didn't you? This type of object memory is a remarkable skill that allows children to learn far more in the first five years of their lives than they ever do for the rest of their lives. Before going to school, children learn by seeing *tangible* objects identified by their parents. The pictures are registered in their minds, never to be forgotten. After entering school, however, children are called upon to learn *intangible* letters, numbers, words, and symbols. Because it is not in picture form, intangible information does not automatically register in the mind. As a result, what was automatic before entering school becomes a lifelong struggle for many people.

Unfortunately, names fall into the intangible category. I have created a system to combat this problem by making names tangible, and thus, far easier to learn.

There are four steps involved in my names-and-faces system.

1. LISTEN, UNDERSTAND, AND PICTURE. Most people are very poor listeners and, as a result, have difficulty remembering names after introductions. By training yourself to be a good listener, you will begin to register names quickly and easily. After hearing a name, process it in your mind and make it tangible so that it can be visualized as a picture, like a dog or a cat. Certain names, like Fawcett, automatically conjure up a picture in the mind (a dripping faucet). Names like Barnes, Coates, and Rose benefit from similarly tangible images. More complicated names are what I call "zip names," those that contain several syllables. A zip name can be visualized by saying the name slowly and listening carefully to what each syllable sounds like. The name Kwiatkowski, for instance, is pronounced "quiet-cow-ski." It is easy to picture a quiet cow skiing.

2. FIND AN OUTSTANDING FEATURE ON THE PERSON'S FACE. This skill is easy to master quickly. You might select distinguished

lines on the forehead, a big nose, a mustache, or one of many other features that attract your attention.

3. CONNECT THE PICTURED NAME TO THE OUTSTANDING FACIAL FEATURE. For example, the picture for the name Ponchatrayne is "punch-a-train." Now, let's assume Mr. Ponchatrayne has very distinguished lines on his forehead that remind you of a railroad track. Picture his name by imagining that you are punching a train off the tracks on his forehead. Such pictures cause an impression on the mind that is easily recalled when you see the person again. You can repeat this visualization process for the first name along with the second name, and, with some practice, you will become successful at remembering both.

4. REMEMBER THE NAME AND NEVER FORGET IT. The person's name, outstanding facial feature, and the picture you see on the face must be recorded and reviewed weekly until you are certain you know the name. In this manner you can review hundreds of people in just minutes, much like meeting or seeing a person again and again. Repeated recall assures success.

When you fully embrace and apply this system, you will never again be stuck having to apologize for your forgetfulness.

–27–

MAKE YOURSELF MEMORABLE

NICHOLAS BOOTHMAN

Nicholas Boothman is the author of three books: How to Make People Like You in 90 Seconds or Less, How to Connect in Business in 90 Seconds or Less, *and* How to Make Someone Fall in Love with You in 90 Minutes or Less. *Renowned for his colorful presentations, the* New York Times *calls him "Dale Carnegie for a rushed era."*

What good is meeting someone for the first time, creating a favorable impression, and establishing a rapport if they've utterly forgotten you two days later?

To make yourself memorable, start by taking a look at the signals you send off unwittingly.

1. ATTITUDE

More than anything else, your attitude determines how people feel about you when you first meet. Choose a "useful" attitude—upbeat, welcoming, and enthusiastic.

2. CHARM

Be charming rather than alarming. Make eye contact, if only for a couple of seconds—this signals that trust is in the air.

3. SMILE

Here's a way to smile with genuine enjoyment. Practice saying the word *great* over and over in a mirror using crazy voices until you feel like a giant idiot or you crack up, then say it under your breath to yourself as you approach people. I guarantee you'll be smiling. A smile sends a signal that you're happy and confident.

4. BODY LANGUAGE

You should appear open and relaxed. Rather than crossing your arms over your chest, go literally "heart-to-heart" with the other person—point your heart toward theirs, which signals that you're not going to harm them.

And of course it goes without saying that you'll be a total turnoff if you don't act politely and follow up when you say you will. Above all, don't try too hard—another big turnoff

Another, more concrete way to make yourself memorable involves using intentional "cues":

VISUAL CUES

If you wear great clothes, you make it easier for people to conjure up an image of you. People tend to remember high-quality accessories or someone who is consistently well groomed.

CHARACTER CUES

Wearing one deliberate, consistent, predictable accessory provides you with a character cue. A fresh flower in your lapel, a bow tie, or Larry King suspenders are all character cues. I always wear red shoes—since 1972! (As a former fashion photographer I can get away with it.) People will say, "The guy in the red shoes is coming back again this year." And others still remember me. Do err on the side of discretion.

SOUND CUES

Take a tip from unforgettable megastars like Madonna, Oprah, Bono, and Liberace and give yourself a single-word name or nickname.

PHYSICAL CUES

Physical cues are less subtle than visual or verbal ones. Think of Johnny Carson's golf swing, Sir Winston Churchill's V-for-victory gesture, or the centuries-old thumbs-up/thumbs-down gestures that became symbols for Siskel and Ebert's movie reviews.

TALKING IN COLOR

Finally, there's one more very effective way to make yourself memorable faster: by peppering your conversation with vivid figurative language. Here's what I mean. When Warren Buffett, a genius at what I call "Talking in Color," was asked how he enjoys his job, he replied, "I tap-dance to work." That's Talking in Color. He engaged the senses and the imaginations of his listeners. Abraham Lincoln talked about the "ship of state"; Martin Luther King, "the mountaintop." Songwriters do it all the time; so do great writers—it makes them memorable. It was the language of the great prophets, like Jesus, Buddha, Mohammed; they told stories and created images that stick in the imagination forever.

A simple way to learn how to Talk in Color is by using what I call "i-kola." That stands for "is kind of like a . . ." When you need to describe something, come up with a picture in your mind: "I'm kind of like an ocean—sometimes calm, sometimes stormy," or "My best friend is kind of like a cup of coffee—he's warm and always gives me energy." When you talk in images, you immediately involve other people's emotions and senses.

Facts and figures fade fast but images can last forever. So put on your best smile, pick a cue, and have fun, because now when you meet new people, you'll make a memorable impression—fast.

MIND

–28–
UNLEASH YOUR CREATIVITY

SCOTT A. JONES

Scott A. Jones is widely known for creating the voice mail used around the world. He is a prolific inventor and entrepreneur. He has created music recognition and discovery, robotics, and mobile technologies products and services that have touched the lives of billions of people.

Many of us have bursts of creativity. Here are some ways to increase the frequency of those bursts and learn to tap into your creative genius on demand and under a deadline. Usually the biggest obstacle is just getting started.

BE KNOWLEDGEABLE IN AT LEAST ONE DISCIPLINE
Whatever area your brain is exploring, you'll need to have a grasp of the basic concepts involved. Albert Einstein knew a lot about physics, math, and philosophy before he came up with the theory of relativity.

MINIMIZE DISTRACTIONS

Clear the deck so that you can focus your energies on the area in which creativity is needed. Completely unplug yourself from your phones, computer, e-mail, television, radio, and any other distractions from people and pets.

GET IN THE PROPER FRAME OF MIND

Sometimes this might involve a walk outside or a trip to a local beach, library, or hilltop. Or it might mean sitting in a room alone and concentrating solely on one simple object, thus blocking out all of life's endless distractions. In my twenties while at MIT, I often took a half day to go "invent" at Walden Pond, near the spot where Thoreau was inspired well over a century earlier.

PICK A TIME THAT WORKS FOR YOU

A different time of day, such as late at night or early in the morning, may provide the proper no-distractions situation. Another great time for creativity is during airplane trips, when most of life's built-in distractions are temporarily suspended.

TINKER

Dedicate a space in your home or office where you can spread out gear that may get your creative juices flowing.

GREEN-LIGHT IDEAS

Capture your ideas on a notepad, voice recorder, white board, or even video camera. In these sessions there are no bad ideas. You can go solo or involve one to six people who must have a positive attitude and, preferably, who inspire you (and the group). The goal here is to get a laundry list of many good ideas from many sources. Try to include people with a different perspective from yours. Sometimes this will help you and them see problems from a different angle or perhaps upside down or inside out!

SPEW, SORT, AND SIFT

Now that you have started getting your ideas down, try reorganizing the ideas. Don't feel paralyzed by not having all the pieces identified or the perfect words chosen. By sorting and sifting through them, sometimes other ideas bubble out of the process. Sometimes you zoom in or out. Sometimes you go in a different direction.

COMBINE IDEAS

The more you know, the more likely you are to be able to combine seemingly unrelated elements to find a solution.

STAY FLEXIBLE

Experts in a field sometimes think there is only one way to solve a problem. They are almost always wrong.

I THINK WHAT BEN WOULD SAY

Another technique for finding inspiration might involve imagining how Benjamin Franklin or some other inventive person would address your problem—if he had all the knowledge available to you today.

GET OUTSIDE YOURSELF

It is absolutely essential to find new ways of viewing problems (and solutions). Some simple techniques for learning to do this include exposing yourself to new things or trying to perform normal tasks in new ways. For example, try eating with your other hand, walking backward carefully from one room to the next, driving a different route to or from work. Doing something (anything) differently every day gets you in the habit of stretching your behaviors and keeps your brain from becoming complacent and making mind-confining assumptions about how things are supposed to be done. Keep creating new neural pathways in your brain.

LET AN IDEA INCUBATE

While you work on something else, your brain will keep on trying to come up with a solution to your original problem.

BE OPEN TO "EUREKA" MOMENTS

Archimedes "discovered" fluid displacement when he stepped into a bathtub.

THINK BIG

Once you've come up with some good ideas, step back and think about how to make the box bigger.

—29—

DO MATH IN YOUR HEAD

ARTHUR BENJAMIN

Dr. Arthur Benjamin is professor of mathematics at Harvey Mudd College, in Claremont, California. He is the author of Secrets of Mental Math: The Mathemagician's Guide to Lightning Calculation *and* Amazing Math Tricks. *In 2005, Reader's Digest called him "America's Best Math Whiz."*

The art of doing math in your head, quickly and accurately, is a process of *simplification*. The problem may seem hard at first, but you gradually make it easier and easier, until all that remains is your answer.

When we learned math in elementary school, we were taught to calculate from right to left. But if you want to do math in your head, it is easier to work from left to right. Working left to right is also important if you want a good mental *estimate* of your answer. For example, it is more important to know that your answer is a little bit over 800 than to know that your answer ends in 1. Most people who work with numbers on a regular basis instinctively work from left to right.

ADDITION

Let's do 567 + 324 without writing anything down. Starting with 567, begin by adding 300, so the problem simplifies to 867 + 24. You now have an easier problem to solve. Starting with 867, add 20 so the problem becomes 887 + 4, which equals 891.

SUBTRACTION

Subtraction can also be performed from left to right. Let's subtract the numbers from our last problem: 567 − 324. Starting with 567, subtract 300 so the problem simplifies to 267 − 24. Then after subtracting 20, the problem becomes 247 − 4, which equals 243.

The last subtraction problem wasn't too bad, because the digits of the first number were all bigger than the digits of the second number. The next problem looks harder because the second number has larger digits. Try 1234 − 795. When large digits are being subtracted, we can turn a difficult subtraction problem into an easy addition problem. Starting with 1234, let's first subtract 800, to get 434. But we intentionally subtracted 5 too much. So we add back 5 to get 434 + 5, which equals 439.

Now let's try 1234 − 567. Begin by subtracting 600: 1234 − 600 = 634. But we have subtracted 33 too much. So our scary subtraction problem becomes an easy addition problem: 634 + 33, which is 667.

MULTIPLICATION

Let's start with 6 × 57. Working from left to right, we know that 6 × 50 = 300, and 6 × 7 = 42. Add those together and we get 342.

Here's one where the addition is a little harder: 7 × 29. We know that 7 × 20 = 140 and 7 x 9 = 63. Add these together: 140 + 63 = 203.

Alternatively, you might find it easier to treat 29 as 30 − 1, and do 7 × 30 = 210, then subtract 7 × 1 = 7, to get 210 − 7 = 203.

When multiplying two-digit numbers, there are often many different ways to do the same problem. Let's do the problem **29 × 21** four different ways:

The *addition* method: By thinking of the number 21 as 20 + 1, we get 20 × 29 = 580, and 1 × 29 = 29. Add these numbers: 580 + 29 = 609.

The *subtraction* method: By thinking of the number 29 as 30 − 1, we get 30 × 21 = 630, and 1 × 21 = 21. Subtract these numbers: 630 − 21 = 609.

The *factoring* method: By thinking of the number 21 as 7 × 3, we get 29 × 21 = 29 × 7 × 3. First calculate 29 × 7 = 203 (like we did earlier), then multiply this by 3, to get 203 × 3 = 609.

The *magic* method: Round each number so that you end up with 30 × 20 = 600 and 9 × 1 = 9. Add these together to get 609. When multiplying two-digit numbers, you can use this method if the first digits are the same and the second digits' sum is ten.

DIVISION

Division is the only operation you are taught to do from left to right, but there are often ways to simplify a division problem. For instance, to do 147 divided by 5, I find it easier to double both numbers and get 294 divided by 10, to get 29.4.

Here is an example that works for multiples of 5: to divide 62 by 25, multiply both numbers by 4, to get the simpler division problem 248 divided by 100, which equals 2.48.

—30—

RELAX

RODNEY YEE

Rodney Yee teaches yoga classes around the world. He has created and starred in more than twenty-five instructional yoga videos and is the author of two books, including Moving Toward Balance: 8 Weeks of Yoga with Rodney Yee.

D o you ever find yourself daydreaming? Do you sense your mind drifting away from what your body is doing? This constant separation of mind and body denies you the ability to fully appreciate and live in the present. And if you don't embrace the present, you'll never be able to relax.

The philosopher and educator J. Krishnamurti said that we need to harness all of our mind, heart, and body into the present moment to produce intelligent, skillful action. Similarly, achieving such harmony will allow you to relax. So, how do we do this effectively?

In yoga, we harness our minds through our body and breath. A simple way to channel your energy is to spontaneously ask yourself throughout the day, "What are my legs and feet doing?" Try planting your feet firmly on the floor and feel the connection they make to the ground. As you root your feet, notice your breath travel from your nose, down your back, and into your legs. Let this single inhalation release any binding pressure inside your neck and head. As you exhale, push the breath out from your rooted feet, through your legs, and up your body and notice how relaxed you become in your mind and heart.

Experiment with your posture throughout the day. Break your tedious physical habits by finding different ways to stand, sit, and move. Next time you are waiting in line, subtly shift your weight to the left, to the right, to your toes, to your heels, and then back into balance. Play with finding and falling out of your physical center. All day long, be conscious of your physical being and focus on the natural flow and ease of your breath. With an attentive posture and easy breath, mental and physical stress are less likely to lodge in your mind and body.

As you consciously look inward, toward your mental and physical being, you may be surprised at how relaxed you are; even your idea of relaxation is improved. To go beyond your original concept of relaxation, you must be willing to delve into unknown body sensations and unmapped mental territories. To do this, lie on your back with legs straight, eight inches apart and relaxed, so your feet naturally fall to the outside. Place your arms down by your sides, with your hands eight inches from your hips, palms facing up. Close your eyes and scan your body from the top of your head to the soles of your feet. Continually be aware of all body sensations. Slowly you will train yourself to relax deeply and yet stay mentally awake and present.

As your state of relaxation deepens you will become more receptive and clear. This will allow you to observe the flow of your breath and notice how your breath moves more evenly in the body. The entire body is like a sponge for the breath; it easily receives the vibrations and nutrients of your breathing. As you are observing your breath, begin to feel how smoothly and evenly you can draw it in. With your body increasingly relaxed, begin to slightly deepen your inhalation and exhalation. Pause slightly at the beginning of your inhalation and at the end of your exhalation. During these pauses, notice how quiet and peaceful the body becomes. From the depth of that quietness, continue your cycle of breathing. To end the exercise, bend your legs, roll to your right side, and sit up slowly.

By practicing this exercise a little bit every day you will become more in tune with your breath and with deeper levels of relaxation. This conscious state of relaxation will begin to permeate the rest of your day.

Remember: Your center, your innate peace, and your innate joy are always available to you. Now that you know how to access them, it's time to unleash them.

–31–

CONCENTRATE

JOEL FISH

Dr. Joel Fish is a sport psychologist who has worked with

countless professional and college sports teams.

He is the director of The Center for Sport Psychology

in Philadelphia and the author of

101 Ways to Be a Terrific Sports Parent.

high level of concentration—the ability to channel attention in a specific direction and maintain focus despite distractions—is necessary to perform at a high level in everyday life, no matter the task at hand. You are bombarded with stimuli throughout the course of a day, and if you are unable to filter out all the sights and sounds constantly swirling around, you will never be able to pay attention long enough to complete any undertaking. This is true of a child in preschool trying to put one block on top of another, the high school student trying to solve a math problem, or the employee trying to write a report before a deadline.

The art of improving your concentration can be accomplished quickly:

1. IDENTIFY PATTERNS

People tend to believe they have either good concentration skills or poor concentration skills. But the reality is that most of us focus well in certain situations and less well in others. Identifying your own concentration patterns is the first step toward developing a game plan to improve your concentration. Do you tend to have good concentration during your first hour at work after a good night's sleep? Does your concentration tend to be at a high level when you're working out in the gym with a particular friend? On the other hand, does your concentration waver in the morning if you are anticipating a meeting with your boss later that day? Do you tend to have trouble sustaining your focus at the gym if you're working out alone?

2. PRACTICE

Practicing with focusing techniques can improve the level of your concentration and help sustain it. Here's a powerful exercise you can use to increase your ability to consciously control where you *choose* to focus your attention:

> *Sit in a chair and have someone give you five commands regarding where to focus your concentration. For example, have someone say to you, "Choose to look me in the eye. Choose to feel your left foot on the floor. Choose to listen to the sound of the ventilation in the room. Choose to listen to my voice. Now choose to feel your right foot on the floor." Then repeat this exercise with ten commands.*

People have tremendous powers of concentration and focus, but only when they are motivated and when they *choose* to channel their attention in a specific direction. Once you master the ability to choose to focus your concentration in a controlled setting, you can apply that skill to everyday life and thereby improve your concentration at home, at school, at work, and anywhere else you wish.

3. IDENTIFY DISTRACTIONS

When we try to block out a distraction, it only becomes more of a roadblock. Conversely, when we acknowledge a distraction, we can then *choose* to shift our attention back to the task at hand. So you need to identify the things that interfere with your concentration. Do you become distracted by loud noises? When someone is watching you? When the room is too hot or too cold?

Once you've identified your particular distractions, train yourself to pick up the signals that your body gives you when you are starting to get distracted. Do you begin tapping your foot? Do you find yourself doodling? Humming under your breath? When you notice your body signaling you in this manner, don't say to yourself, "I can't think about that. I can't think about that." Instead, say, "I am getting distracted again by the music. That's okay I know what to do. I will choose to focus on the task at hand."

In sport psychology, when an athlete improves his or her concentration by 3 to 5 percent, the athlete is considered to have a "mental edge." If you immediately adopt the plan described here, you can improve your concentration by 1 percent a week starting now and quickly gain a mental edge that will make you more successful at whatever challenge you tackle.

—32—

THINK ON YOUR FEET

BOB KULHAN

Bob Kulhan runs Business Improvisations, working with companies around the country on customized improvisations. He is an adjunct professor of business administration at Duke's Fuqua School of Business and performs with a number of improv groups, including Baby Wants Candy.

Let's face it—whether it be in business (unexpected opportunities, meetings, putting out "fires") or life (greeting surprise guests, driving a car, dating)—we *must* think on our feet every day. Even if we plan our entire day down to the last letter, Murphy still has the ability to enact his law at the most inopportune time, forcing us to adapt in order to execute even the most mundane of tasks effectively.

Thinking on your feet requires a combination of observation and pattern recognition, acquired knowledge and training, and gut reaction.

PRACTICE! PRACTICE! PRACTICE!

Thinking on your feet requires a certain muscle group in your brain to be in good form. And like any muscle, if you don't consistently work it out, it atrophies and gets weak. You must regularly practice thinking on your feet to keep this muscle group as sharp as possible.

TRAIN YOUR BRAIN

- Give yourself time each day to react to life. Work on spontaneity. Strengthen this muscle.

- Study human behavior. Sit in a park or at an outdoor café and people-watch. We are pretty predictable; patterns can be recognized and action can be anticipated. Moreover, study yourself. Find your weaknesses and take steps to convert them to strengths.

- Run through possible scenarios for any given interaction, thereby increasing the speed at which you think on your feet for any circumstance. When you first arrive in a situation, play out how things might unfold. Anticipation will help you react faster.

- Play games like Catch Phrase or Scattergories, which combine intelligence, frame of reference, and memory accessibility with speed.

- Take an improv class. Improv classes train your brain to be more spontaneous and nimble, to make connections, and to be more comfortable taking risks.

STAY LOOSE

Thinking on your feet is not a science. So, don't tense up. There are a million right answers—see which one grabs you, let it come out, and make it work for you. Take a deep breath, relax, and let *you* come out and play!

LOOK FOR OPPORTUNITIES

Too often we run from task to task and miss beautiful opportunities when they surface. It is easy to get trapped inside your head and overlook the present. Stay focused in the here and now. This is where the opportunities to think on your feet await you. So keep your eyes moving, and be aware of your environment as well as the people around you as often as possible.

HAVE CONFIDENCE IN YOURSELF

Fear is one of the top barriers to reacting quickly. Worrying about how others will judge you if you act or react in a certain way will, very often, deter you from acting at all or, at the very least, slow your response time. Besides, if you spend your life focusing on how everyone else *might* want you to behave you will:

1. constantly second-guess yourself
2. lose your individualism
3. miss moments of spontaneity, creativity, discovery, and greatness

Afraid of what *might* happen if you act without thoroughly thinking through everything? Just remember: The mettle of your character is not defined by any one action but by the consistency of all your actions over the course of your life.

If you want to think on your feet, then you not only have to recognize unexpected opportunities when they arise, you also have to hunt them out, train your brain, learn to expect the unexpected, have the courage to react to them, and adapt to make them work for you.

—33—

JUDGE SOMEONE'S CHARACTER

GREG HARTLEY AND MARYANN KARINCH

Greg Hartley and Maryann Karinch are the coauthors of How to Spot a Liar. *Hartley was an army interrogator and an instructor in both interrogation and resistance techniques. Karinch is the author of twelve books, most of which address human behavior.*

First, you must define *character* in your own terms.

In the intelligence world, we determine a set of requirements for each interrogation, which drives how we assess the usefulness of our source. Think of character in this way and make a list of your criteria. A "person of good character" can mean different things to different people.

Second, ask yourself, "Have I ever been wrong about first impressions?" If the answer is "Yes, often," then you know you cannot trust your gut. If the answer is "No, never," then you absolutely cannot trust your gut. If you fall somewhere in the middle, let your gut be your first screening device with a caveat: If you do not trust someone from the start, analyze. If you do, keep your eyes open. Both involve these next elements:

1. Steer away from snap judgments. Many factors can skew your view, such as your connotation of words used by the person, and preconceived notions you have about the meanings of accents, dress, and body language. I call these "filters," and they include prejudice of any kind, including your own feelings of inadequacy that cause you to project attributes onto your source.

2. When you start talking with him, pay attention to how he converses. Is he talking *to* you or *at* you? People who talk *at* you broadcast information. Someone who talks *to* you engages you and follows conversation, discovering tidbits like why you drive a green minivan.

3. Look for what is normal for him in terms of rate of speech, cadence, gesturing openness (e.g., palms up, elbows away from the side), and body positioning. As your gut says, "Do not trust him," look for changes in each of these as well as word choice, blink rate, eye contact, and voice tone. None of these individually tells you he is lying, but they show signs of stress. When people are lying or trying to cover something, these signs of stress will increase.

4. If someone is uncertain as to how she is being perceived or whether you believe her, she will hold her brows raised for an inordinate amount of time as if asking for approval. That can be a sign that you should not trust the story.

5. People naturally open up as they start to trust each other. So if she starts the conversation with her arms crossed or holding some-

thing in front of her, think nothing of it. Even if she continues a closed posture, you can assume it is just her normal pattern. But if she walks away and adopts an open posture with others yet puts up barriers in relation to you—with arms, a table, a bag—all the while telling you how much she likes you, she has integrity issues.

6. Some people can mimic persuasive, open body language and look normal, though nothing could be further from the truth. If you feel especially good in someone's presence after just meeting him, take a break from him for a few minutes. If you wonder what you think is so good about him while you are away, but feel great again in his presence, then he is what I call "glossy." You know the kind. That few minutes away to give you perspective could save you a lifetime of annoyance.

People who are honest keep a consistent baseline throughout conversation. Open body language and physical illustrators that punctuate a person's thoughts at appropriate times are good indicators that he is genuine. By starting with a clean slate, asking yourself what you are looking for in the context of your own values and beliefs, and keeping in mind the above mentioned six elements of analysis, you can spot someone who meets your character criteria.

-34-

SAY NO

TIM DRAPER

Tim Draper is the founder of the global venture capital firm Draper Fisher Jurvetson in Menlo Park, California. He has heard more than 100,000 business pitches from entrepreneurs and funded 0.06 percent of them.

Before you say no, think about whether you are doing so for the right reasons.

1. Understand your mission in life (or at least in work). Make sure your answer (yes or no) is helping you achieve that mission.

2. Understand your priorities. Give the answer that feels right. Make sure you have thought through any repercussions that might come from the rejection.

3. Understand your own motivations. Be sure you are purely motivated (without jealousy, fear, anger, or ruthlessness in your heart) and there is no petty reason for the rejection.

Before you say no, think about whether you need to say no.

1. Is this the right thing for everyone?

2. Does it feel right in your gut? Once you do it, will you be relieved or will you feel uneasy? If uneasy, you might have to do some evaluating of your priorities.

3. How will all the other people involved react? Have a plan for each of them.

Now, here's how you say no:

1. Swallow your own pride. The "no" recipient's ego is at risk here. Keep his ego intact at the sacrifice of your own.

2. Lay out the big picture. Explain why it is in everybody's best interests. If you do it right, the other person will believe it is for the best.

3. Give real reasons why. If those reasons are personal, start with the positive, then work toward what you want and how the recipient doesn't match your ideal model.

4. Depersonalize it: "This is something that couldn't be helped, because . . ."

5. Be decisive, be honest, be polite, be quick. Once you have made the decision, do it. No matter how mean the recipient is, you need to be polite and kind. He is under stress; you shouldn't be. Speedy action will clear the air sooner.

6. Do it now. Delaying a "no" makes it worse for the recipient.

Avoid the following excuses that delay:

1. You need the person to get something done for you before you tell her no. It turns out that in the school yard the two processes are often linked (e.g., "I will do this for you if you do that for me"), but in the work world, they are usually not. If you are going to say no, do it, and suffer the consequences. Often you will find that the two things you thought were linked are not.

2. It will crush the person. In the case that you believe you will crush the life out of the person you are saying no to, you will have to get a little creative. For example, if you were to turn someone down for a job, get the person thinking about alternatives as soon as you can. "There is another job down the street." "I recommend that you try ___. They are a lot more ___ than we are, and they may be looking for someone of your experience and quality."

3. You want to avoid it for a day or two. You want to catch him in a good mood, or on a Friday, or after she's had a chance to discuss it with her mother. Delaying bad news is the worst thing for its future recipient. Bad news should be heard immediately, so that the maximum amount of time can be used to react to it. If someone is going to lose a job, he needs to get back out there as soon as he can. If she is not going to get a loan, she needs to set up her contingency plan as soon as she can. If he is not going to get a date, he needs to move his heart to another.

Ultimately, you will have to develop your own style. And finally, saying yes is usually better.

–35–
OVERCOME GUILT

KEITH ABLOW

Dr. Keith Ablow is a psychiatrist and the founder of livingthetruth.com, *a self-help/empowerment network inspired by his latest book,* Living the Truth: Transform Your Life through the Power of Insight and Honesty. *He is a Fox News contributor and previously hosted his own syndicated daily TV talk show,* The Keith Ablow Show. *In addition to being the author of eight nonfiction books, he is a bestselling crime novelist.*

There are many triggers for guilt—doing someone else harm; letting down loved ones, coworkers, society, your God, or yourself. Maybe you've experienced guilt after telling someone's secret, or being unable to commit to a relationship, or failing to complete a task, or giving up on a dream, or abandoning a diet. Guilt is normal. We're prewired to feel it. My son, six, will sometimes cry when I ask him why he didn't share a toy with a friend. My daughter, ten, apologizes if she forgets to put water in our dog's bowl.

Guilt is generally a good thing, because it grows from concern for the feelings and well-being of others. The ability to feel guilt is deeply connected to the ability to empathize and is part of what's missing from the emotional makeup of sociopaths. Trust me, I've testified in enough murder trials to know.

When we are overly sensitive to pleasing others, however, our normal, healthy guilt circuitry can be inappropriately triggered. We can be so worried about losing affection or support or praise that we feel guilty merely for thinking independently or asserting ourselves or even being fair rather than favoring someone.

So before you can overcome guilt, you must determine whether you have anything to feel guilty about in the first place. That's where my three-step healing strategy for guilt starts:

STEP 1: DECIDE WHETHER OR NOT YOU'VE REALLY DONE ANYTHING WRONG

This step is easier than you might think. Here's the all-important question: Did you actually "steal" something from another person, whether property or time or an idea or trust of which you turned out to be unworthy? If you did, you have something to feel "real guilt" about. If, on the other hand, you are living life your own way and that fact offends someone—like your controlling older brother—then you are experiencing "referred guilt." Like referred pain, referred guilt is actually coming from somewhere else, whether another facet of a relationship or another chapter of your life story.

Not sure which guilt you're dealing with—real or referred? Put yourself in the position of the other party. Would you justifiably feel something had been taken from you? Would you feel hurt? If not, that's a clue that someone else is trying to make you feel guilty to manipulate you. (If it's yourself that you've let down, reassert your self-worth by considering the lapse a learning experience and understanding you're human. Show you care about yourself by trying again—harder this time.)

STEP 2: APOLOGIZE . . . OR NOT

If you've done something that leaves you with real guilt, waste no time. Apologize to the person you've hurt and make amends. Say more about your shortcomings, rather than less. People have much more forgiveness in their hearts than you might imagine, and your own heart will be more easily restored by asking for it. Example: "I planned to call you last week when you were sick, but I didn't. I let myself get distracted with work, as always, when you mean so much more to me. I'm sorry."

On the other hand, if you're a victim of referred guilt, having taken nothing that wasn't yours to begin with, then you have nothing to apologize for. Feel free to explain why you acted as you did, but don't feel as though you need to justify it. Example: "I understand that you want me to call you every day, but some days my schedule is too full, or I just want private time. I hope you understand."

STEP 3: MOVE ON

This is both the simplest and the hardest step: whether you've apologized and made amends or reasserted your independence and made yourself clear, you've done what you could. If pangs of guilt still visit you, let them go without getting lost in them. You'll notice they come fewer and farther between.

—36—

BURY THE HATCHET

DALE ATKINS

Dr. Dale Atkins is a psychologist in private practice in New York City. She has written a number of books, including Sanity Savers: Tips for Women to Live a Balanced Life.

"Bury the hatchet" is a term derived from a Native American Iroquois ceremony in which war axes, tomahawks, scalping knives, and other weapons of the feuding Mohawk, Oneida, Onondaga, Cayuga, and Seneca were buried in the ground to ensure that all thought of hostility would be out of sight—a meaningful act because as humans we are vulnerable to return to earlier behavior, even behavior we want to change.

Most of us have relationships that are fractured. Just as it was difficult for warring tribes to make peace, it is often hard for us to bury the hatchet of long, festering animosity. However, letting go of lingering disputes—even if the other person involved doesn't seem ready—is essential to improving your own health and well-being. No matter how legitimate your pain, anger, and disappointment, holding on to feelings of hurt and resentment creates harmful responses in your body. Intense emotional feelings produce a chemical response in your brain: positive feelings produce chemicals that enhance positive energy and well-being, while negative feelings produce chemicals that contribute to high blood pressure, greater stomach acidity, increased muscle tension, and jaw clenching, headaches, and disturbed sleep. Moreover, holding on to negative feelings harms others. When you are joyful people around you feel at ease; when you are vengeful they feel stressed.

In order to bury the hatchet quickly, you must first embrace the idea that doing so is the right thing for you. Next, you need to accept that doing so is a process, and you must embrace that process, described below, with an unwavering commitment. It is not enough just to decide you are willing; you must also engage in practices that will give you the insight and strength to bury the hatchet and leave it buried no matter what the other person does or does not do.

BEGIN WITH YOURSELF

Ask yourself, "What is my motivation to reconcile?" There are many reasons and you need to be aware of yours. Without a sincere desire to move forward with a fresh outlook, it will be difficult for you to benefit.

PRACTICE AND PREPARE

Relax your body and your mind so that you can visualize the kind of life you want to live. Slowly breathe in and out, focusing on your breath as you alternately tense and relax your muscles. Breathe *in* peace. Breathe *out* love. See yourself as part of a larger world in which this one person and relationship are but a small part of your entire life and no longer require the negative energy you have given them.

SHED YOUR "RIGHTEOUS MANTLE"

The need to be right can prevent you from experiencing a more positive, peaceful life and hinder your effort to rebuild a relationship that may have potential. Sustain your commitment to reconciliation and your own mental and physical health by pledging not to demonize or devalue the other person. It is important to follow through on this in your thoughts as well as in your words and actions.

PHYSICALLY "BURY THE HATCHET"

This may sound silly, but I strongly encourage you to take something that represents the hatchet and physically bury it. Know it is there and buried and vow that in the future you will not engage in destructive thoughts, words, or behavior. Whether the other person chooses to join you in a more positive, healthy, joyful existence is a decision only he or she can make. Fortunately, you have the ability to choose your path for yourself.

Once you have embraced your own clarity and strength, you might be ready to engage in a face-to-face reconnection with the other person. On the other hand, sometimes burying the hatchet without engaging the other person at all is the better part of wisdom. For example, it can be harmful to reenter an abusive relationship, opening the door for continued mistreatment, for the purpose of making peace. And in other cases, the person with whom you would like to reconcile may not be interested. Whatever your specific circumstance, take comfort in knowing that you have buried the hatchet yourself and moved past the past toward a more productive and healthy life.

–37–

IMPROVE YOUR VOCABULARY

ADAM LOGAN

Adam Logan is one of the world's leading Scrabble players.
He won the World Scrabble Championship in 2005.

There are many different reasons to increase your vocabulary. You might aspire to be more articulate in conversation. You might want to read the classics of seventeenth-century drama. You might need to learn the technical terms for a job. Or perhaps you are trying to improve your skill at solving crosswords or playing Scrabble.

1. CHOOSING WORDS

If you need to do well on a standardized test, look for lists of words that the test's creators are fond of. If you want to read old poetry, you should make lists of words you don't know as you go. For building a technical vocabulary, a textbook is a useful source. However, unless you understand the ideas behind the definitions, memorizing the terms is of little use.

2. CARDS OR SOUND FILES?

Most people think of themselves as either visual or auditory learners. If you are a visual learner, like me, I recommend that you make flash cards or use an equivalent computer system. Test yourself by looking at each card for a few seconds. If you know what the word means, check the other side to make sure. Be pleased with yourself (briefly) and go on to the next card. If you aren't sure, look at the other side to remind yourself of the meaning. Repeat the word and its definition softly to yourself once or twice. Once you're done, shuffle the deck and start again. Auditory learners can make a tape, CD, or audio file of their words. Be aware that this has the disadvantage of fixing the order of the words more than flash cards do—you don't want to memorize in order.

3. CONTEXT

We all find it easier to retain information when we view it in context rather than in isolation. For a technical vocabulary, this is easy: you can sort the words by theme. If you found the word in a book or in a poem, you could copy the sentence in which it appears. In cases where the context is not available, you can create one by writing your own sentence using the word. Crossword game players might prefer to sort words by length and letters used.

4. REPETITION

After a few times through your deck of cards, you will be absolutely confident with many of the words. (The more words you have already learned, the faster this will happen.) At this point, you can put these cards in your storage deck. But never assume that you know a word for good; a word that seems completely solid may revert to unfamiliarity if you don't review it for a year or two. A lot of short sessions are better than a few long ones, and it's important to do at least a little bit every day. Many people have a preferred time of day for study, such as first thing in the morning, at lunchtime, or before going to bed. Of course, if you need to learn words quickly, you can do several sessions a day, but don't be surprised if you forget them just as quickly as you learned them.

5. USAGE

Using or hearing your new words in a natural context is the best way to reinforce them; and anyway, if you don't use the words you learn, why are you learning them? So, read the plays you've been wanting to read, talk to experts in the field you're learning about, or just talk to people who have large vocabularies. If you use a new word successfully, that will help—and if you find that you can't, then you know what to review.

-38-

FORM OPINIONS

JESSE KORNBLUTH

Jesse Kornbluth is a former contributing editor of
Vanity Fair *and* New York *and is editorial director of*
AOL. *He founded and edits HeadButler.com and opines*
occasionally on The Huffington Post.

F our days a week, I write eight hundred words about a book, movie, or CD I love. That calls for a lot of reading, looking, and listening. But anyone with a decent work ethic, a modest gift for summary, and a knack for Google can do that. The tricky part is having a crisp, original opinion that makes the review worth reading—and coming up with that opinion against an inflexible deadline.

By "opinion" I do not mean the categorically stupid, ideologically rigid propaganda that passes for thought on cable TV, talk radio, and too many newspaper columns. Wait! I don't necessarily mean all that. But I have your attention, don't I? Why? Because I'm expressing a point of view—a sharp opinion, clearly stated. And that's your challenge: to deliver crisp opinions of your own and to arrive at them faster.

You may think that, when a topic is introduced, the trick is to think quickly and talk swiftly. For most of us, that's not a reasonable short-term goal. There are famous exceptions, of course. Oscar Wilde thought fast, and the instant quip became as much his signature as the well-made play. But today's best-known opinionmeisters have cadres of writers; despite Stephen Colbert's and Jon Stewart's long history of stand-up comedy and improvisational theater, it's impossible to know where their staff ends and they begin.

The first path to faster opinions is to be like the professionals. Prepare for this moment so you don't have to think, you just stand and deliver. It's a paradox—briskly delivered opinions are a long time coming. So don't feel badly about adopting my interim approach: filling your head with a reservoir of quips.

Doing so is a simple matter. You just have to read—and underline, the better to remember—and watch and listen. Great opinions can be found in every genre of literature and culture; your task is to identify people worth quoting. And then you simply steal their wisdom—as T. S. Eliot said, "Minor poets imitate, great poets steal"—or, if you prefer, name the source and show off

Talking about employment opportunities? Try this: "I stand with Hunter Thompson: 'A job? But how would I make any money?'" Or, when the conversation turns to the latest sex scandal, here's a handy-dandy quote from Samuel Johnson: "No man is a hypocrite in his pleasures." Whether you cite your source or not, you'll want a few dozen of these.

History is a great resource; an opinion that puts a current situation into perspective is always a genius move. But it might be more fun, in this age of instant everything, to go to the Web. Yes, for blogs. Not the ones you already visit or that express views you agree with—you want an opinion that's just the opposite of yours. The whole point of reading unfamiliar views isn't to be converted, but to be provoked, to get a fresh reaction.

Do enough wide-awake reading, watching, and listening, and you'll be well on your way to developing a critical attitude toward life. You might find yourself assuming that everything you read or see is a lie—at the very least, a fudged truth. And then you may ask yourself: What's really going on here? Who benefits? How does this affect me? Those questions are the spur to meaningful opinions. And given that most people sleepwalk through life, any opinion you offer on a topic freighted by received opinion will be as refreshing as grapefruit sorbet.

Very soon, you'll find yourself surrounded by people who want to catch every pearl of your wit and wisdom. You will be tempted to drone on. Don't. If asked for more, dissemble. Or, better, quote Voltaire: "The secret of being a bore is to tell everything." Which is, come to think of it, an opinion you can trot out anytime, anywhere—instantly.

–39–
OVERCOME FEAR

BARBARA OLASOV ROTHBAUM

Barbara Olasov Rothbaum is a psychologist at Emory University School of Medicine in Atlanta, Georgia, and a professor in the psychiatry department. Dr. Rothbaum is head of the Trauma and Anxiety Recovery Program (TARP) at Emory and the founder of a virtual exposure therapy company called Virtually Better Inc.

Fears are common, but when they start to interfere with your life—usually because of avoidance of situations that trigger fear—it's time to address them. The best and fastest way to overcome fears is to face them head-on through exposure therapy. This involves confronting your fear in a controlled and systematic manner. You want to teach your mind and your body that what you fear won't actually happen, thereby reducing your fright even during exposure to the fearful stimulus.

In order for a therapeutic exposure to be effective it must be:

1. LONG ENOUGH for your anxiety to decrease while you are still in contact with the fearful stimulus;

2. REPEATED over and over so that you can convince your body that it is safe;

3. FOCUSED UPON THE PRECISE SITUATION OR ELEMENT THAT YOU FEAR. If you are scared of driving a car, just being a passenger won't help.

There are several ways to expose yourself to your fear:

• In your imagination

• In real life

• Using virtual reality

When you confront your fears, it is important to remember a few things:

1. Though it is natural to want to eliminate anxiety, we are hardwired to feel anxiety and fear in certain situations. You can confront your fears successfully even if you are scared all the while.

2. If you confront your fear for long enough and you are not under realistic threat (no one is pointing a gun at you), your fear *will* decrease. Stay with it until your anxiety diminishes. If you run away while still scared, it will reinforce that there is something to be scared of.

3. Anxiety is normal and almost no one can tell how anxious you are feeling, even if you feel that your heart is ready to pound out of your chest.

4. Performance is actually enhanced when you are under an optimal level of anxiety and stress. When your body is a little wired you tend to be on your toes, be more energetic, be more responsive, and think faster on your feet.

5. Don't believe everything you think. Just because you are scared, it doesn't mean there is a realistic threat. Even if you fear that you look scared or silly, you probably don't.

6. For some of the more "global" fears, such as the fear of terrorist attack or of being shot, it can help to remind yourself that these are low-probability events and are unlikely to happen to you or anyone you love. Remember the old Buddhist adage that "attention enhances" and focus your attention on something else.

7. Learn to recognize your fear "themes" and then you can use shortcuts to remind yourself that you will be fine and that your anxiety will come down. For example, you may immediately jump to the conclusion that because your heart is pounding when you are driving on the highway, you are about to have a heart attack or stroke and should pull over immediately. You can later remind yourself when you are driving on the highway that your pounding heart is not dangerous and will pass even if you keep driving.

When you are ready to begin your exposure therapy, utilize a systematic approach. Start by creating a list of things you fear and be very specific, rating how scared you think you would be under specific fear stimuli, from 0 (no anxiety at all) to 100 (maximum anxiety). For example, if you fear driving, your list might look like this:

ANXIETY	SITUATION
50	Driving alone in your neighborhood
60	Driving alone to the grocery store, parking, driving home
70	Driving with a friend to the mall, parking, driving home
80	Driving alone to the mall, parking, driving home
90	Driving with your spouse on the interstate for five exits and driving home
100	Driving alone on the interstate for five exits and driving home

Using your list, expose yourself to progressively more stressful stimuli. Stay with each step until your anxiety decreases before moving to the next step. If you find a step to be too stressful, add an in-between step to help you make the transition. Put yourself on a fear exposure schedule and stick to it. Make a record of your attempts, including your level of anxiety and how long you exposed yourself to your fear, and note any changes in your level of anxiety as you progress. Utilizing this method, you will be able to eliminate your fears, one by one, in a systematic manner. Most important, no matter how afraid you are, don't leave your worst fears to fester.

-40-

READ AND COMPREHEND

HOWARD STEPHEN BERG

Howard Stephen Berg is the world's fastest reader, the author of many books, including Speed-Reading the Easy Way, *and the creator of a number of speed-reading products.*

Each day more information is published than in all of human history through the year 1800, yet the average reading speed is only two hundred words per minute. No wonder staying on top of information seems so hard. Most people read like third graders, one word at a time, starting with the first page of the book. A more efficient way to read is to employ my four steps of scope, schema, scan, and skim.

SCOPE

Thumb through your text starting at the beginning and moving toward the end at approximately two to five seconds per page. You are not reading but looking for the main idea or big picture. Determine your text's boundaries. Look for things like sections, chapters, or other features. Also, decide if time, location, people, topic, theme, or issue defines the text. You are drawing a circle around the material you will be focusing on later.

SCHEMA

Now thumb from the rear of the text back toward the beginning, searching for what the author has done to make important points stand out—things like the use of illustrations, captions, and time lines. Search for terms that are set apart using bolding, colors, sidebars, and other textual effects. Look for the "back material" provided by the author, such as glossaries, summaries, and questions. You now can easily spot the important information that the writer has taken the time to mark off for you.

SCAN

Starting at the beginning, loosely read the text looking for what the writer considers important based on your use of schema. Pay close attention to the headings and subheadings to see how the material flows, and, again, watch for text that is **bold,** *italic,* or treated in other distinctive ways. Look for questions and summaries as well. Set up a two-column table, and in column one list all the new vocabulary, names, dates, headers, and questions.

SKIM

During the scanning process you identified and set up a table of what you need to know. Now you will learn the details to these items while skimming. From the rear of the text begin reading toward the beginning, finding information that provides the details you need for your list in column one of your table. Focus most of your attention on the new vocabulary, names, dates, headers, and questions. In column two of your table write down in your own words (do not copy) the meanings of the words, the importance of the individuals, the significance of the dates, the four key points for each header, and the answers to each question. You now have a list of all the essential information you need to learn, and can quickly use memory techniques to retain it.

PUTTING IT TOGETHER

There are more steps using my method, but they take less time to complete. Ever drive home during rush hour and take a longer route to get home sooner? You did not care if you traveled farther if it took less time to arrive at your destination. The same is true with my reading secrets. There are more steps, but they take less time while empowering you with better comprehension.

BODY

–41–
FALL ASLEEP

MICHAEL BREUS

Dr. Michael Breus, a.k.a. The Sleep Doctor, is a clinical psychologist, WebMD's sleep expert, an AOL wellness coach, and the author of Beauty Sleep: Look Younger, Lose Weight, and Feel Great Through Better Sleep.

If you fall asleep "before your head hits the pillow" or in less than five minutes, you are likely sleep deprived. What we all want to do is try to fall asleep within fifteen to twenty minutes of lights-out. Here are a few simple rules to follow for successful sleep:

YOUR BEDROOM

Ask yourself:

- Is this an environment conducive to sleep?
- Is it clear of clutter?
- When you walk in, is it a place of calm tranquillity?

If your answers are no, here are a few quick tips for faster sleep:

1. Change the bulbs in your bedside lamp to 40 watts, put a night-light in your hallway and in the bathroom, and consider an eye mask. Why? Light tells your brain it is morning and you stop producing melatonin, one of the main hormones that help you fall asleep.

2. If there is any noise that disturbs you (TV, snoring bedmate, street noise), eliminate it with ear plugs or a sound machine. Why? Data suggests that we stay in the lighter stages of sleep when we hear certain noises.

3. Is your sleep system (mattress, pillow, sheets) doing a good job? Is your mattress more than ten years old? Is your pillow more than eighteen months old? Are you uncomfortable? Do you wake with back pain or a stiff neck? If the answers are yes, you may need a new sleep system.

4. Clean up! Clutter in the bedroom can be cumbersome when you get up at night and reminds you of stressors (kids, work, bills).

5. Is it too hot or too cold? Research shows that the optimal sleeping temperature is between 68 and 72 degrees, so try to get there. This may be more difficult to do depending on your geography.

YOUR BODY

- Are you exercising regularly? Regular exercise has been shown to promote deep sleep and shorten the time it takes to fall asleep.

- Do you have issues with pain? See your doctor and get the pain under control to get a better night's rest.

What can you do?

1. Begin a regular exercise program under the guidance of your doctor, but try not to overdo it. There is conflicting data on exercise at night, but if that is your only time to do it and it relaxes you, then go for it.

2. Consider a warm to hot bubble bath before bedtime. The bubbles form a layer of insulation and keep the water hotter longer. The heat will raise your core body temperature, and when you get out of the tub your temperature will fall. This drop in temperature is a signal to your brain to begin the production of melatonin. So take a hot bubble bath and then enter a cool, dark bedroom.

YOUR BRAIN

Do you have trouble "turning your mind off"? If yes, it's likely because the first opportunity you have to really think about things is when you finally lie down. It is okay to think, but not to ruminate. Continuing to think about stressful events, times, or thoughts will cause autonomic arousal, meaning your body will react, and when it is reacting it is not falling asleep.

What can you do?

1. Consider a "worry journal." Write down your concerns with one answer to each problem, then put it away for the night, clearing your mind for sleep.

2. Consider meditation or relaxation. Learn progressive muscle relaxation.

3. Consider distraction. Try counting backward from 300 by 3s. It is not easy and is so boring that it should put you to sleep.

–42–

WALK

MARK FENTON

Mark Fenton is a former member and coach of the U.S. National Racewalking team, author of the best-selling The Complete Guide to Walking for Health, Weight Loss, and Fitness, *coauthor of* Pedometer Walking, *and a leading consultant on community designs, engineering, and policy initiatives to create more walkable, bicycle-friendly communities.*

Want to start showing up at the grocery store sweaty, or make a habit of arriving at meetings out of breath? Well, probably not. But you should, as long as it's the result of having walked faster to get to your destination. The easy part is explaining *how* to turn just about any walk into a workout. The bigger challenge may be convincing you it's worth the effort (and the occasional quizzical stares it will earn you).

So here are ten ways walking faster works to your advantage:

1. EFFICIENCY. Get places faster, which means *walking* to your destination becomes more of an option. In a world of pricey gas, the two-step taxi sounds like an ever better option.

2. CONSCIENCE. As speed lets you walk a little more and drive a little less you reduce your carbon footprint and contribution to global warming. What could be greener?

3. GRAVITY. A faster stride looks more serious and smart. A purposeful pace gives you presence.

4. RIGHT OF WAY. Panhandlers, vendors, and those with street surveys always give way to the speediest pedestrians and focus on the slowpokes.

5. SAFETY. Yup, even muggers won't think it's worth the effort to chase you down once you pick up the pace.

6. QUIET. Absorb nature, observe architecture, listen to the rhythm of your own footsteps—with a fast enough pace even your most long-winded walking partner will be too out of breath to disturb your serenity.

7. HEART HEALTH. Experts urge all adults to get at least thirty minutes of *moderate* activity (think 1.5-mile walk) every day to reduce the risk for chronic disease and an early death. But bump up the intensity even just a few days per week and you can reduce your risk for heart attack or stroke significantly more.

8. WEIGHT LOSS. Stroll three miles in an hour, burn about 240 calories. Step it up to a brisk four miles in an hour, and you'll churn through closer to 400 calories.

9. FITNESS. Want to play soccer with the kids or climb stairs without getting winded? Faster walks will provide aerobic conditioning that you simply can't get with casual ambling.

10. GREAT GAMS. A brisk walk is sure to give you more muscular legs, from shapely calves to toned thighs and firm glutes.

Okay, you're sold on the idea of hasty walking, but you're still not ready to head out in public with the exaggerated swagger of a competitive racewalker. Instead, just make these four simple biomechanical adjustments—lessons gleaned from the racewalking gait that carries competitors at speeds of eight miles an hour and more—and you'll be on your way to improved calorie burning and transportation efficiency.

1. STAND TALL. No slouch in the shoulders, forward lean from the waist, or excess sway in your back. Cue: Keep your eyes on the horizon, and don't let your chin drop.

2. FOCUS ON QUICKER, NOT LONGER, STEPS. Yes, your stride gets longer as you walk faster. But that shouldn't be your goal; let it happen naturally. Instead, concentrate on taking faster steps. Cue: Count how many steps you take in twenty seconds; shoot for more than 45 (that's 135 steps per minute, or roughly 3.5 to 4 miles per hour).

3. BEND YOUR ARMS. Hold your elbows at right angles so your arms can swing more quickly; target a quick, compact arm swing. Cue: Hands should trace an arc from alongside the waistband on the back swing, to chest height (no higher) in the front.

4. PUSH OFF YOUR TOES. Consciously push off your toes and generate as much boost as possible at the end of each step. Cue: Feel like you're showing someone behind you the bottom of your shoe at the end of every stride.

Once you've got this down, take on one more challenge. Think of friends who'd benefit from some exercise, and take them out for a walk. And you've got my permission—the first few times, let them set the pace.

-43-

RUN

JUSTIN GATLIN

*Justin Gatlin is the 2004 Olympic gold medalist
for the 100 meters and the 2005 Double World Champion
gold medalist at the 100 and 200 meters.*

Whether you are in a race, trying to impress your significant other, or being chased, here's what you'll need to do to run fast.

THE PREP

For starters, you need to dress the part. I suggest a lightweight tank top and running shorts. If you're the stylish type, you may want to wear a fancy Lycra top and bottom set that formfits to your body, which will help give the appearance that you're fast. Complete your outfit with a hot colorful running shoe, or even a competitive racing spike if you're running on a track. And please wear ankle-length socks; if you wear those ugly socks that come up to your calves, I wouldn't even want to be *seen* racing against you.

Most important, always remember to hydrate your body prior to running. You should be fully hydrated approximately two hours before your activity. There are many good sports drinks that promote energy and recovery, but you can never go wrong with water. There are also several good energy and protein bars that are widely available, and you should include these in your training regimen. You can consume energy and protein bars up to one hour before your activity. Due to the vast amount of calories burned during any physical exertion, it's important to replace nutrients after each workout.

THE START

A good start is essential to running fast—especially when you're sprinting—helping you to control your energy and reach maximum speed. Today, all sprinters use starting blocks, a Z-shaped apparatus that lies on the running surface. A starting block acts as a solid base to help propel your body forward at the beginning of the race. One foot is placed more forward on one side of the block, while the other foot is placed farther back on the opposite side of the block. Though you may not be involved in a formal sprint, the same techniques will apply. When setting up at the start line, relax your body. Slowly raise your body to the start position and make sure your weight is equally distributed between your arms and legs.

THE DRIVE AND TRANSITION PHASES

The Drive Phase covers the first 15 to 30 meters of your movement. At the sound of the gun or "go" command, don't pick up your head and arms. Instead, sweep them from the ground. Upon leaving the blocks, keep your head down with your chin tucked to your chest, and allow your movement to be led by your head and the tops of your knees. Your first five steps should be identical and explosive. You will then cross over into the Transition Phase of the race, during which your body transitions from the Drive Phase to acceleration. This is the most important aspect of running fast, and it requires patience. Yes, you have to have patience when accelerating. You don't want to reach the natural upright running position in one stride—instead, transition to upright using a progressive motion over the course of 5 meters. This upright position will last throughout the race, allowing you to run at maximum speed. At this point, your arms and legs should follow a smooth but powerful cycling motion.

BREATHING

You should establish a consistent breathing pattern when running to allow your muscles to receive a consistent amount of oxygen. Try breathing every four strides throughout the race. You may feel better breathing every three strides; whichever rhythm you're comfortable with is fine. However, avoid panting. It will only cause your body to tighten, which will cause you to fatigue sooner.

THE FINISH

Once you're within 10 meters of the finish line, do not look at the line but past it. Don't change your current running pattern by getting too excited. Relax and maintain your form. As you get closer to the end of your race you may lean at the finish line or simply run through the line. Leaning is used primarily when you're in a close race and trying to beat your opponent (or your pursuer!) by a hair.

These are the basic tools I've used to become a successful sprinter, and I hope they will be helpful should you, too, feel the need for speed. Try it—it's a rush!

–44–

STOP BLEEDING

CARLOS VARGAS

Carlos Vargas is the cutman for ESPN's boxing reality show The Contender. *After a career as an amateur boxer, he took up his role as a cutman in countless professional fights and martial arts events. He maintains his day job as a firefighter in Northridge, California.*

As a cutman in boxing, I get only one minute in between rounds to stop the bleeding, and I am allowed to use little help. I approach the injured fighter, wash the cut with a clean, wet towel, apply one of the approved medicines (coagulants prescribed by a doctor to licensed professionals) to the cut with a swab or sterile gauze pad, hold the pressure for about three to forty-five seconds, release, and apply Vaseline to the area to prevent the opponent's leather boxing gloves from tearing the cut apart any farther. I continue this process until the match is over or the ring doctor stops the fight due to the severity of the cut. Stopping the bleeding fast is crucial to the outcome of the match. Many fights have been lost due to the cutman not being able to stop the bleeding.

An adult has approximately five quarts of blood in his body and, needless to say, it is not good to lose it. It is very important to stop bleeding fast. These tips apply whether it is a cut caused by a punch in a boxing match or an injury sustained in everyday life:

1. Wash the affected area with a clean towel or cloth and cool water.

2. Take notice of the amount of blood pouring from the wound. This will tell you how severe the cut is and what kind of treatment is needed, as well as whether you should take the injured person to the hospital. Severe bleeding would be a bright red color and gush out steadily, maybe even squirting with every heartbeat. In this case, bandage the cut or wound with a clean compress pressure bandage (gauze), and take the person to the hospital or call 911.

3. Apply pressure with a sterile cloth directly on the wound or cut, but not too hard as it could add to the injury. By applying pressure, you will stop the flow of blood to the injured area.

4. If you are headed to the hospital, keep the injured part of the body from moving in transport.

In severe life-or-death emergencies when you cannot make it to a hospital, you can use a tourniquet, a method of stopping blood flow to a particular area by wrapping a cloth or rope above the injury and making a knot tight enough to stop the localized blood flow. In some instances when you cannot get the tourniquet tight enough, you can place a stick on top of cloth and spin the stick to create a tight enough bandage to stop the blood flow. Think of it as similar to shutting off a faucet. A tourniquet should be used only as a last resort to save a life because by putting pressure on the veins and arteries, it cuts off blood flow to that body part, which in a worst-case scenario may have to be amputated due to lack of blood flow for a long period of time.

A final thought drawn from my experience in boxing. I have seen a cutman carrying cotton swabs on his ear, in his mouth, and sometimes in his pocket. It is important to keep all wounds free of dirt and germs, so keep all swabs, pads, and medicine in a sterile state until it is time to use them.

By following these steps, you, too, can be a "cutman" within your own home, or at work if the occasion demands it.

-45-

RECOVER FROM SURGERY

MARK SCHLERETH

Mark Schlereth played guard in the NFL for twelve seasons (1989–2000) with the Washington Redskins and the Denver Broncos, winning three Super Bowls. Schlereth endured twenty-nine surgeries, twenty on his knees. He is a football analyst for ESPN's NFL Live.

It took twenty-nine surgeries to receive my MBA in "speedy recovery." Now I'm going to help you graduate from the "surgical school of hard knocks." We've all heard the saying "No pain, no gain." And I mean P.A.I.N. Follow these four steps and you will be back on your feet in no time. Always make sure you have exhausted all nonsurgical measures before deciding to go under the knife.

PERSEVERE

Push yourself through the mental pain that accompanies every part of rehabilitation. Quit your whining, leave the pity party behind, and get to work! "A mind is a terrible thing to waste," but let me tell you, it can be a terrible thing to listen to as well. Fear of the unknown can keep us from pushing our body to the necessary limit for a quick recovery. When your mind says that your body has had enough, don't listen. I promise you your mind will say "uncle" before your body. Listen to your body; it will tell you when it has had enough. If you can push through the pain and discomfort, you will be well on your way to getting back on your feet.

ASK

Believe it or not, a speedy recovery begins even before you slip into that well-ventilated surgical gown. Talk to your doctor about any presurgery workout programs that he or she would recommend. The better shape you are in BEFORE surgery, the quicker your recovery will be. Believe me, I know. Make sure the area surrounding your surgical site is as strong as possible, leading up to your trip to the hospital. This will help limit the muscle atrophy following your procedure. The less atrophy, the faster you can get your muscles firing on all cylinders during your rehab.

ICE

Postsurgery you're going to have to apologize to your dog, because for the next four weeks ice must become your new best friend. Icing your surgically repaired area helps reduce effusion (fluid buildup), deaden pain, and speed the healing process. Ice in twenty- to thirty-minute intervals and always allow the iced region time to return to normal body temperature before starting again. This usually takes several hours, but as soon as it is back to temp grab that ice bag and begin again. Repeat this process as often as possible. Adopting an aggressive attitude toward your icing schedule will also help you wean yourself off addictive pain medications more quickly.

NO REST

Sure, you're allowed to rest a little, but avoid becoming a couch potato at all costs. The more sedentary you allow yourself to become, the harder it will be to get back to an active lifestyle. Digging yourself into the couch like an Alabama tic after your procedure will only allow the swelling and soreness to set in more deeply and add significant time to the recovery process. Movement and exercise pump oxygen-rich blood throughout your body and will quickly put you on the road to mental and physical recovery.

If you can endure the P.A.I.N., your friends will soon be asking you how you recovered so quickly. While I would never wish surgery on anyone, at least if you have to have it you will now know how to get back on your feet ASAP.

—46—

CURE A STOMACHACHE

CRAZY LEGS CONTI

> *Crazy Legs Conti is the subject of the documentary* Crazy
> Legs Conti: Zen and the Art of Competitive Eating. *He
> is Major League Eating's eleventh-ranked competitive
> eater in the world and holds world titles in beef brisket,
> pancakes, bacon, French-cut string beans, and Twinkies.*

Is there anything more quaint than a small child's shaky voice saying, "I have a tummy ache"? It is a vision of Norman Rockwell's *Doctor and Doll*. An adult stomachache, however, feels more like Edvard Munch's *The Scream*. What can you do to quickly cure the rolling ocean of stomach rumbles or the sharp pain in the belly that has you bending over in agony? As a competitive eater, I have consumed voluminous amounts of food (thirty-eight doughnuts) in very short amounts of time (eight minutes) and, while digesting, gauged the effect on the stomach (a dead-center compact sour ball of hurt). Ranked or not, we are all gustatory gladiators and long to return to the table as soon as possible. Nothing prevents a world record, or simply a dinner date, like a stomachache.

The following three methods will get you back to the table fast.

DIGESTIVES

Dense or rich foods you've regretted ingesting respond well to the digestive treatment. Skip drugstore tablets and grocery store biscuits. Also, ginger ale is good for neither stains nor stomach-aches because these days it's mostly corn syrup. Fake sugar will only ferment your agony. The carbonation will cause burping, which feels good, like a pressure valve releasing, but stick to selt-zer, not soda, to enable short-term belching relief. Early versions of the golden soda contained ginger, the plant, hence the common belief in the ale's restorative powers. What you actually need is fresh ginger, sliced, boiled, and then served as tea. Digestives derived from roots, herbs, and mints have long been a remedy for overindulgence.

Additionally, many are mixed with alcohol. The French diges-tif (Cognac, Armagnac, Calvados) is the most common; however, I favor the Italian Fernet-Branca, which has a vague medicinal taste, hints of root beer, and overtures of dirt. Limiting your intake to three ounces won't get you inebriated, but will alleviate your gurgling belly. Simply quaff, sit comfortably, and wait. After twenty minutes, you should notice your stomach settling. If not, drink another three ounces and continue to do so until you are pain-free (or drunk). One July Fourth, I was musketball-loaded with twenty-three and a half Nathan's hot dogs and buns when a beautiful woman asked me to ride the Cyclone roller coaster. I sipped Fernet-Branca until my stomach found the courage.

FLUIDS

We take for granted the advantages of modern plumbing, but would be wise to acknowledge the flushing mechanism in the human body. Get your system moving with lots of water. Drink a half gallon of water and the stop-and-go rush-hour traffic of one's lower intestines will find log-flume-like speedy relief in no time. If peristalsis (muscle contractions in your digestive tract) is the culprit, expulsion can be the hero and water the catalyst. I spent an evening in Alaska, my stomach wrestling with eighteen reindeer sausages. However, after the water method, by morning, I was able to mush on to pancakes and bacon (four and a half pounds in ten minutes).

THE MIND

Even if your eyes are bigger than your stomach, your mind is bigger still. Your stomach has the storage space of a small puddle, but your mind, with a greater capacity than the Grand Coulee Dam, can never fill up. Putting all your mental energies toward something else, getting distracted, and ignoring the physical pain will often make it go away. It's mind over stomach matter (I often daydream of salad) and it works for pro eaters and casual diners alike.

These methods will quickly lead your Jackson Pollock–splattered insides to the calm waters of Monet's lilies.

Bon digestif!

-47-

CHOOSE A HEALTHY SNACK

KERI GLASSMAN

Keri Glassman is the author of The Snack Factor Diet *and president of Keri Glassman, A Nutritious Life, a nutrition counseling and consulting practice in New York. She is the founder of KeriBar, a nutritional snack bar company, and creator of Skin Appetit, a food-based skin-care line.*

B y now you've probably heard the buzz about snacking—it's good for you! However, it's not just about snacking; it's about choosing the *right* snacks. And when you are on the go, you are likely to choose the *wrong* ones.

Choosing the right snack starts with preparation. Keep your office, home, car, and bag stocked with healthy snacks. It's easy to grab a bag of high-fat potato chips or a sugary candy bar when you don't have anything else to eat. Having access to healthy snacks will ensure that you snack the right way.

When choosing a snack, look for the following qualities:

- PORTION-CONTROL: Snacks are meant to *fuel* you, providing you with just enough calories to keep your energy up and metabolism high, but not so much that your body stores the excess as fat. Aim for 100 to 160 calories per snack. Some people need one snack per day, others four. Listen to *your* body and eat accordingly.

- NUTRIENT DENSE: Get the most bang for your buck—the most nutrition for the least number of calories. A 1-ounce bag of pretzels provides you with nothing but calories, so you keep eating because you don't feel full. For the same calories you could eat a fiber cracker with a layer of peanut butter and benefit from fiber, protein, and healthy fat. Plus, these nutrients will keep you satisfied. When looking for a nutrient-dense snack, ask yourself, "Is this snack providing me with fiber? Protein? Healthy fat? Vitamins? Minerals?" If the answer is "Just calories," steer clear. Likewise if the answer is "Protein but high fat," or "Fiber but high sugar." Shoot for snacks containing the following:
  Fiber (at least 3 grams)
  Healthy fat (e.g., almonds, peanut butter, olive oil, avocado)
  Lean protein (e.g., plain yogurt, turkey, edamame)

  Aim for a combination of these traits and keep in mind that these foods will also provide you with vitamins, minerals, and phytonutrients (health-promoting, antioxidant-rich compounds found in many fruits, vegetables, and other foods).

- SATISFY A CRAVING: Have you crunched on celery hoping to avoid eating pizza? Eating around a craving makes you overeat calories from other foods or overconsume what you crave later on. Instead, pinpoint the craving and choose a nutrient-dense, portion-controlled alternative. Craving pizza? Go for piz-zettes—a fiber cracker topped with 1 tablespoon of marinara sauce and 1 tablespoon of reduced-fat mozzarella cheese and microwaved for 15 seconds. Yum!

Other things to keep in mind:

- Ask yourself if you are really hungry and listen to your body!
  - Your *hunger quotient* (HQ)—a rough measure of how hun-gry you are—should always be somewhere between slightly hungry (6) and slightly satisfied (4) on a scale of 1–10, 1 being stuffed and 10 being starved.
  - If you're *not* hungry but rather bored, stressed, anxious, or tired, try taking a nap, reading a magazine, or doing some deep breathing. If you need to put something in your mouth, try a cup of herbal tea or a glass of water with a squeeze of lemon. Sometimes you can mistake thirst for hunger.
- Avoid foods with added sugar, partially hydrogenated oils, or anything artificial, and always pick foods with the smallest number of ingredients.

FAST FAVORITES:

- Celery sticks filled with 2 teaspoons of natural peanut butter (provides protein, fiber, and healthy fat)
- ½ cup of nonfat cottage cheese mixed with 10 chopped almonds and ground cinnamon (provides calcium, healthy fat, and protein)

- 6 ounces of nonfat plain yogurt with 2 tablespoons of ground flaxseeds (provides healthy fat, protein, and calcium)
- Soy chips—1.3-ounce bag (provides protein)
- 1 cup of steamed edamame (provides protein and fiber)
- Carrots and celery with 3 tablespoons of hummus (provides protein and fiber)
- Air-popped popcorn sprinkled with 2 tablespoons of Parmesan cheese (provides fiber and calcium)
- 1 cup of vegetable soup (provides fiber)
- 1 fiber cracker with 1 teaspoon of natural peanut butter and dark chocolate shavings (provides fiber, protein, and healthy fat)

–48–

IMPROVE YOUR POSTURE

JANICE NOVAK

Janice Novak is the author of Posture, Get It Straight!:
Look Ten Years Younger, Ten Pounds Thinner and
Feel Better Than Ever. *She is a wellness consultant and
teaches posture workshops around the world.*

Your posture—the way you stand, sit, and move—has a profound effect on your health and appearance. No matter how bad your posture is or how long you've had poor posture, it is never too late to improve it. Some of the benefits you'll reap from improving your posture:

- Prevent/eliminate back and neck pain
- Instantly slim your midsection by an inch or more and help flatten your belly
- Peel years off your appearance
- Create a more commanding appearance

• Improve athletic performance and decrease your chance of injury

You have good posture when, from a side view, your ear, shoulder, hip, knee, and ankle line up vertically. This instant alignment technique will have you standing straighter immediately:

1. Stand with your feet six to eight inches apart. Your knees should be neutral, not locked.

2. Pull in your abdominal muscles as if you were trying to zip up a tight pair of pants. Think of pulling your belly button toward your back. Don't hold your breath.

3. Next, lift the front of your rib cage up as if a string were attached from your breastbone to the ceiling, pulling you up.

4. Pull your shoulder blades back toward your spine, and then press them down as if you want to tuck your shoulder blades into your back pockets. This will help straighten rounded shoulders.

5. Gently stretch the top of your head toward the ceiling, as if a string were pulling you upward.

6. Now march in place or walk around for a few minutes, trying to keep your rib cage lifted, your abdominals pulled in slightly, and your shoulder blades pulled back. Make sure you are moving your limbs naturally.

Over the next several weeks, every time you find yourself slumping, realign with the above steps. Every time you pull your abdominals in, shift your rib cage up, and pull your shoulder blades back and down to strengthen the muscles that support good posture.

The next step is to further strengthen the muscles that will prevent your shoulders and rib cage from rounding forward and your belly from hanging out.

TOTAL POSTURE IMPROVEMENT EXERCISE:

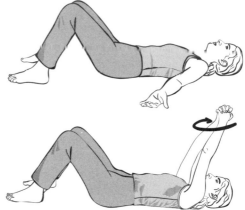

1. Lie on your back, knees bent, feet flat on the floor.

2. Place your arms at your sides at a forty-five-degree angle to your torso.

3. Face the palms of your hands toward the ceiling.

4. Inhale. As you exhale, gently press your lower back toward the floor. Don't force anything. Then press the middle of your back into the floor, then your upper back. Think of pressing your whole spine gently into the floor.

5. Next, press the backs of your shoulders into the floor. As you do this, you should feel every muscle in your back contract.

6. Stay for a count of ten, without holding your breath, then relax.

7. Clasp your hands and stretch your arms toward the ceiling. Draw big, easy circles—five times in one direction and then five times in the other—which will allow all of the upper- and mid-back muscles to relax.

8. Repeat steps 1 to 7 three times.

–49–

DRESS SLIMMER

JOE LUPO AND JESSE GARZA

Joe Lupo and Jesse Garza are the founders of Visual Therapy, a luxury lifestyle-consulting firm based in New York. The two stylists cowrote Nothing to Wear?: A 5-Step Cure for the Common Closet *and* Life in Color. *They are style experts on Oprah.com.*

I f you want to dress slimmer with speed, embrace the following mantra: Everything begins with an expertly edited closet. Treat your closet like your MP3 playlist and make every garment one of your own personal greatest hits. In other words, your closet should be full of clothing that fits, feels good on your body, and makes you feel confident when you are wearing it. By editing your wardrobe, dressing to create a sleek silhouette will be as simple and efficient as speed dialing.

BEGIN WITH THE SKIN

A luxurious garment's appeal can be totally lost if your underpinnings are ill-fitted. So get your hands out of those discount bins full of leopard-print, jeweled bras and take the time to get measured for the correct size. A bra that is too small or too large is bound to create unwanted bulges and spillage. Aim for coverage and lift to appear thinner and younger and create smooth lines. Don't be afraid of undergarments that offer a little bit of assistance. There are countless body slimmers that smooth out—they are called foundation garments for a reason.

CREATE A COLUMN

Fashion addicts are crazy for black. However, don't shy away from other dark neutrals, such as navy, charcoal, and chocolate. You can use these colors to create the desired monochromatic "column" effect. By dressing in one shade from head to toe (think quintessential fashion maven Jackie Kennedy Onassis), your body will look long, lean, and seamless. A great way to accent this ensemble is to add one piece that pops, such as a colorful scarf, a great bag, or a pair of gloves.

MATERIAL MATTERS

Extra layers are often thought to downplay the appearance of a little extra loving underneath. But unless you are preparing for an Antarctic expedition, avoid piling on too many garments. If you do layer, opt for lightweight, fitted pieces. Knits with stretch should reign supreme in your wardrobe. A knit gives and takes in all the right places, allowing you to simultaneously achieve restriction and feel at ease.

SWEATERS/TOPS

The clavicle and shoulders are two of the sexiest and thinnest parts of a woman's body and should be accentuated. An open neckline created by a scoop- or V-neck top is universally flattering because it reveals a bit of skin and elongates the neck. Take your shirts to a dry cleaner—most offer alteration services and can put darts in the back of a shirt, which will create the effect of a narrower waistline. Sweaters should also skim the body, but avoid creating a tight, sausage-like look.

DRESSES/SUITS

A woman in an asymmetrical, bias-cut dress oozes modern sex appeal. Don't wear skirts that hit at mid-calf or at the ankle, as these pieces will make your legs look heavier. Choose a straight skirt or one that hugs your curves before it flares.

PANTS/JEANS

Jeans tend to be the toughest garment to fit perfectly. To create an hourglass effect, the jeans' legs should be slim enough to hug your shape. Select denim with 2 percent stretch. Mid-waisted jeans are good with heels for a slimming, leggy look but they can flatten your butt. Low-rise jeans (not thong-baring low!) are more flattering for curvy silhouettes (those people with a flat stomach, hips, and butt). Baggy jeans will only make large bodies appear even larger. And remember, never wear pleats when trying to look trim.

COATS/JACKETS

Outerwear should fit close to the body and buttons should close securely without pulling. A single-breasted coat nipped in at the waist creates a desirable shape. A higher armhole will give a slimmer look, and a little stretch goes a long way.

STEADFAST SILHOUETTE

For women of any size, a tunic worn with a slim pant is a classic go-to ensemble. Pair one, or a long cardigan, with a slim tank and leggings. Belt the outfit inside and let the cardigan flow, or belt the entire look. The final creation results in an appearance of long legs and a tiny waist.

HEELS

When it comes to achieving a sinewy form, heels are the ultimate women's accessory. The additional height not only helps to create a long, lean silhouette but also makes a dramatic fashion statement.

Looking slimmer with speed is all about knowing what you need and want before you shop and get dressed. Buying smart—not paying more—is the key to achieving both comfort and sexiness. Starting out with the right attitude and knowledge will bring you one step closer to looking slimmer faster. Own your style, be proud of your body, and wear your clothes with conviction.

–50–

CHOOSE AN OUTFIT

STACY LONDON

Stacy London is the host of TLC's Fashionably Late
with Stacy London *and the cohost of TLC's* What Not to
Wear. *She is a stylist to many celebrities, a* Today *show
contributor, and the coauthor of* Dress Your Best.

How many times have you flung open the doors to your closet
and thought, "I have nothing to wear"? With a few simple
steps, you can make getting dressed for any occasion an easy,
quick, even enjoyable, experience.

PURGE THE CRAP

Get rid of all clothes that are not currently in rotation. This includes
clothes that no longer fit (they are emotional baggage you don't
need) or don't fit well (make your tailor your best friend!), senti-
mental items you got from family members (put that crocheted
cardigan Grandma made you in a hope chest, please), and
Halloween costumes! Separate gym clothes from actual clothing.
(If you're having trouble putting together an outfit for the gym,
you probably need more help than I can give you in this chapter.)

Store clothes that are for another season. Removing all the clutter allows you to see what is in your closet.

ORGANIZE THE ESSENTIALS

Once you have pared down to the clothes you regularly wear, these three levels of organization will help you make sense of your wardrobe:

1. Organize by type: pants, shirts, dresses, jackets, and skirts. Keep suits together as if they were a single item of clothing. If you have the closet space to do so, separate formal wear entirely.

2. Organize each of these categories into color, mixing in prints closest to the color that makes up the majority of the print.

3. Organize your accessories (i.e., shoes and bags) along the same principles. (I'll say a word about jewelry later.)

UNDERSTAND THE PIECES OF THE PUZZLE

Suits and dresses are the easiest outfits to build as they are, in a sense, ready-made. Suits simply require the proper underpinning (shells or shirts) and dresses can be worn on their own or with a sweater or jacket. Separates get more complicated.

1. SUITING should always be a neutral color (black, white, cream, khaki, navy, gray, brown) or a neutral pattern (meaning a pattern that is visible only close up: pinstripe, glen plaid, windowpane). You will get the most wear out of your suits if you can change the underpinnings or break the pieces up and wear them with other separates.

2. DRESSES can be neutrals, colors, or prints. Each one will have its own personality depending on its shape and fit.

3. TOPS AND SKIRTS should be worn in colors that flatter your skin tone and prints that match the stature of your frame.

4. (NONSUIT) JACKETS invite creativity. They can change the tone of an outfit and are great for transitioning from day to evening. Look for metallics and prints to add punch to neutral items.

5. (NONSUIT) TROUSERS should be neutral in order to get the most use out of them. (That's probably why you haven't worn those electric-purple pants since 1985.)

MIX AND MATCH

1. Neutrals go with everything and one another.

2. Balance is key. If you wear a bright-colored or bold-patterned top or bottom, anchor it with a neutral- or solid-colored top or bottom. Never let a color or pattern overwhelm an outfit. It's *you* who wears the clothes, not the other way around.

3. You can mix patterns in an outfit. Make sure one plays the leading role and the others are supporting players. If the patterns are significantly different but all are in the same color palette, they can often work together.

4. Balance is also important when choosing the shape of the clothes in your outfit. If you wear a voluminous top, wear a narrower bottom, and vice versa.

5. Your accessories don't have to *match*, but they have to *go*. Decide whether your accessories will complement or contrast with the outfit. If you wear a bright-colored dress, pair it with a neutral shoe. If you wear a gray suit with a white shirt, try adding pop to the outfit with something bright like a red bag.

6. Last, a word about jewelry. If your goal is to get dressed faster, don't overdo it. Use one strong focal piece as opposed to lots of little pieces. Use an accessory where it will be seen, not where it will look cluttered. A strong earring works with a simple top. A multi-layered necklace works with a deep V-neckline.

–51–

STYLE YOUR HAIR

SALLY HERSHBERGER

Sally Hershberger owns hair salons in Los Angeles and New York. Her high-end clientele includes countless celebrities, from Meg Ryan to John Mayer. Her new line of hair products is available at Walgreen's.

Styling your hair can be a daunting task, especially when you are in a rush. People often get frustrated too soon into the mission and then either give up completely or end up looking overstyled. While throwing your hair into a ponytail sometimes seems like the only option, with a few easy-to-follow pointers almost anyone can have great style, even when on the go.

Whether your hair is short or long, the most important thing to take into consideration is its texture. Get to know your hair—is it fine or thick, coarse and unruly, limp, normal? Next, what's your end goal—do you want a natural look or something more daring? These two basic questions should help you identify what product you'll need, which often is half the battle.

Let's start with some rules that apply to everyone. First,

embrace your natural style as much as possible. The less you try to fight what your hair wants to do naturally, the easier (and therefore faster) it will be to style it. Next, evaluate whether you need to start from scratch or you can rework a specific section (or sections) of hair by lightly wetting them down and blow-drying them to reactivate the style. A spray bottle is the easiest way to wet hair down quickly and in sections. Often, just one part of the hair needs to be restyled, which can save you a lot of time. Finally, use product to help achieve your look, but use it *sparingly*. One of the biggest mistakes people make is using too much product. Hair ends up looking greasy or overstyled—which is never a good thing! Remember, you can always add more product if you need to, but once it's in, it is hard, if not impossible, to go back.

STRAIGHT HAIR

After towel-drying hair, apply a light-hold styling gel or cream from root to tip, then comb through. If using a volumizing spray, which you may want to do if your hair is naturally limp, it should be sprayed directly at the root of the hair immediately before blow drying to help add body. Now, assuming your hair is more or less straight, you can save time by letting your hair mostly air-dry, then simply concentrating on the top sections of hair, leaving the underneath sections as is. Also, make sure to use a round brush with vents (and preferably one made of boar bristles), which will allow for the air to flow through the brush and back to the hair, drying it faster. If you have a couple of extra minutes, run a flat iron over the same top sections you just blew out, in order to smooth and refine the look. Finish with a shine spray to lock in the style and lock out humidity.

CURLY HAIR

Always start with a product that helps to eliminate frizz and builds a barrier against humidity. To generate frizz-free curls on the go, apply product and then twist small sections of hair (one-half inch to one inch wide, depending on how tight your curls are) in your fingers, and then air dry or, to speed up the process, place your hair in a diffuser, an attachment that can be slipped onto the end of a standard blow-dryer. Even if you have only five minutes, this will get the process started and work to set the curls' shape. Another trick that is especially great for those on the go is to braid the hair loosely and then let it air-dry. When you let the braid out you will have a pretty, natural sort of "ropy" wave to your hair.

–52–

ZAP A ZIT

KATIE RODAN

Dr. Katie Rodan is the cocreator of Proactiv Solution, the bestselling acne treatment system in the United States, and the cocreator of Rodan + Fields Dermatologists. She has a cosmetic dermatology practice in Oakland, California, and is an adjunct clinical associate professor of dermatology at Stanford University Medical Center.

The most unwanted visitor, the zit, taunts you with its power to ruin a potentially great day. It's red, it's throbbing, and it feels like a huge headlight in the middle of your face. No matter how much makeup you apply to camouflage this blight upon your otherwise perfect face, you are certain that every person you see will be staring straight at it with laser-focused precision. And you can count on a zit appearing at the absolute worst time—the day of a big job interview or much anticipated blind date, or even spoiling a wedding or senior prom. It may help you to know that acne vulgaris, the medical term for zits, happens to the best of us (even dermatologists), afflicting 90 percent of the population during either the teen or adult years. As an equal opportunity offender, acne doesn't discriminate on the basis of skin type, ethnicity, or socioeconomic background. So since most of us are doomed to get it, how can we quickly and effectively deal with this intruder?

AN OUNCE OF PREVENTION

Acne is a complicated process that silently occurs deep inside any one of the ten thousand pores on your face. Contrary to popular belief, diet and dirt do not cause acne.

Genetics and hormones trigger acne. The process begins with the formation of a plug that entraps sticky oil, allowing for bacterial overgrowth and, finally, provoking your body's inflammatory response. Because this process takes place over days or weeks, treating just the zit is too little too late. It would be like brushing a tooth after a cavity had formed. Daily treatment of your entire face is your best insurance policy for pimple prevention. Using a combination of acne-fighting medicines, such as benzoyl peroxide, sulfur, and salicylic acid, as part of your ritual ensures the most effective way to proactively stop breakouts by stopping the process before the zit surfaces.

911

Even if you are faithful to a daily routine of topical acne medicines, there is always the one that got away. Pimple panic sets in when you see and feel that "fifty-pound" knot on your chin, knowing it could persist for a week or more. What is the gold-standard treatment, or the method used by movie stars who get a big zit during filming? It is a cortisone injection delivered by a skilled dermatologist, which will shrink that pimple, usually by the following morning. Unfortunately, this is not a do-it-yourself-at-home cure, but if you have a dermatologist whom you regularly see, call her office and the understanding receptionist will no doubt fit you into that day's schedule.

If the dermatologist isn't an option, here is my advice:

1. Don't pick or squeeze! Injury to the skin will worsen the inflammation, causing the zit to last much longer or, potentially worse, result in a permanent dark mark or scar.

2. Lessen the inflammation and swelling by applying ice, or even a drop of Visine, which "gets the red out." A dab of 1 percent hydrocortisone, available without a prescription, may also do the trick.

3. Next, cover the pimple with a high concentration of benzoyl peroxide (6 to 10 percent) or a mask containing sulfur, which may be left on overnight to shrink its size.

4. Conceal with a lightly green-tinted makeup (which is widely available), followed by a liquid concealer that matches your skin tone (avoid the waxy, pore-clogging concealers in a lipstick-type tube).

5. Set with a loose oil-free powder.

Now you should be ready to face the day with confidence.

–53–

APPLY MAKEUP

LAURA MERCIER

Laura Mercier is a celebrity makeup artist and the founder and creator of Laura Mercier Cosmetics and Skincare, a global brand of makeup and skin-care products.

Whether you are sleepy or simply rushed, you don't always have enough time for makeup. Whether you have fifteen minutes or five, this is going to help you leave the house feeling better.

TOOLS

To start, get organized. Always have your makeup ready so that you don't waste time searching for your tools in the morning. Double your essentials; have one set for travel and one set for your bathroom, so that they are always at the ready.

PRIORITIES

If you have to run out of your house unexpectedly, you want to have been finished with the essentials. So test yourself. If you could wear only one product, what would you choose? Start here. And follow the priorities in order of whatever is essential to make you most confident. For some women it is the eyes because they look sleepy without eye makeup. For others it is the eyebrows or the lips. If bad skin is your issue, your first priority is to cover your skin. In this case, your eyes and lips become the accessories. If you have perfect skin, skip foundation. If you have any skin issues at all (dark circles, puffiness, broken capillaries, or pimples), start with your skin.

If you are doing a complete face, here is your priority list:

1. SKIN

Make sure you have a good skin-care routine because you will struggle with the texture of makeup if you have skin that isn't moisturized. If you have time for only one thing, make it a moisturizer all over your face except for the eyelids. Once complete, move onto the issues. If you have a localized break-out but an even skin tone, skip foundation and go straight to concealing dark circles with a concealer and covering pimples with a camouflage-type product.

If you are a foundation devotee or you have uneven skin tone, don't cover your whole face. Go directly to your issues. Determine where you need foundation most and put the foundation on those areas only. It is best to apply overall foundation with a sponge, but if you are just doing localized areas, use your finger to blend. If you need or want full coverage, always use a sponge because you are in danger of applying too much when using your finger. When you don't need much coverage, you can stick with a tinted moisturizer in place of foundation. Because it is lighter you can use your fingers to apply.

On cheeks, use your fingers to apply a cream blush or a cream or gel bronzer for speed.

2. POWDER

Always finish with a setting powder. This avoids getting makeup on your clothes and will ensure that it stays on your face all day. Apply it to key places—around nostrils, the forehead, and the chin—and when almost nothing is left on your puff, do the cheeks. Make sure you don't see any powder element lying on the surface of your skin. If you see it you have applied too much.

3. EYES

If you have thick dark lashes, you can skip eyeliner and mascara and head straight to eye shadow. If you have light eyes, start with eyeliner. Always have your eyeliner sharpened so you don't struggle with a dull or low pencil.

- EYELINER. A pencil is faster than a liquid. Start at the top and do a more subtle line on the bottom. If you are in a huge rush, forget about lining the bottom.

- EYE SHADOW. When it comes to color, cream is the quickest. It applies without crumbling, so there is no danger of getting it on your clothes.

- MASCARA. Always have tissues handy and wipe the excess mascara off the tube before using it so it doesn't get clumpy. You can always add mascara, but it is difficult to remove, so use the building technique. Coat your lashes lightly the first time and then keep going until you get the desired effect.

- BROWS. If you have good eyebrows, don't touch them. If they need work, start by brushing them with an eyebrow brush, using an eyebrow pencil to fill them in, and, if you have more time, brush eyebrow powder on top.

4. LIPS

Always apply lip balm after kissing your bedmate good night. This will ensure that your lips are soft and ready for lipstick in the morning. A coat of lip gloss is the quickest. If you are not a gloss person, stain your lips quickly by applying a lipstick with your finger, and skip lip liner. Then put lip balm on top of the color stain. If you have a bit more time or your lips are your focus, always have a neutral-colored lip liner on hand and apply this first so that you don't drag the lipstick to the edge of your lips. Then fill in with a lipstick.

LOVE

-54-

RECOVER FROM A BREAKUP

RUE McCLANAHAN

Rue McClanahan is an Emmy award–winning actress and the author of My First Five Husbands . . . and the Ones Who Got Away. *She is best known for her role as Blanche Deveraux on* The Golden Girls.

When it comes to the emotional fallout from a breakup, an ounce of prevention is worth a pound of cure. What does that really mean for you? Well, let's talk about your options:

1. Don't get involved in the first place. That's a surefire preventive tactic. Sadly, it won't work. So scratch that.

2. You do the breaking up and let the other person get over it. Always worked for me . . . but it's not always going to happen this way.

3. Don't get *really* involved, i.e., don't let your guard down, even if you fall in love. Hmm, I think we're onto something here.

You see, the real tough question is: How do you recover faster when you've *fallen hard* for someone and that someone unexpectedly *dumps you?* Ah, yes. There's the rub.

Say you're in a serious affair, maybe even thinking marriage. You're deeply in love. You think he is, too. And maybe he is. You've been together long enough to be intimate, cook for each other, go out, maybe every night. You think you've found the right guy. When you fight, he apologizes as often as you do. He sends you notes. You give each other personal, lovely, heartfelt presents. You plan surprises for each other. This could be it! And then, seemingly out of nowhere, he tells you he needs to move on. How can you possibly let him go without him taking your heart with him?

Oh, I've been there, my darlings. Big-time. My young heart got, if not completely broken, woefully cracked. And it healed very slowly, very painfully.

In the midst of my pain, however, something quite suddenly dawned on me. I remember the very night. This man who had hurt me was meeting me to talk about things, when I felt this *click*, a total shift in outlook, a realization that I possessed a very powerful tool. What was this miraculous *click?* It was a voice inside me that said, "I'm separate from him. I'm impervious to being hurt. I don't need him to want me. I feel clear. Whole. My own woman." What do you know? Talk about a sense of security! Safe! In charge! On top of things!

And then he drove up and we talked, and we actually continued seeing each other for several more months. But never again did I feel at his mercy.

Did that *click* ever save me again? Many times, though it didn't mean I'd never feel the pain of a breakup. There was one particular affair that devastated me. For some reason this particular breakup brought back the memory of when my first husband left me pregnant, feeling helpless and desperate, while I was still in love with him. But this later heartbreak lasted only two weeks—that's what we call "normal"—while the first one had tortured me for twenty-five years. Now, that was sick. I can tell you with certainty that the difference was that *click*. My ability to move on and recover quickly came from not being needy . . . that's all! If you're needy and he dumps you, you will suffer.

So, how do you get over a breakup faster? *Don't go into the relationship needy!* This works on all levels, from casual dating to marriage. Love him, yes—but, girl, love yourself first and foremost! By doing so you'll empower yourself, so much so that you won't even be able to be devastated because you'll know that you're still you, still lovable, even if he does move on. God bless him . . . let him move on! And move on yourself, lady! Believe me, you're worth it. And believe me, it works.

–55–

RECOVER FROM A LOSS

DAN GOTTLIEB

Dr. Dan Gottlieb is a practicing psychologist and family therapist. He is the host of Voices in the Family, *which airs on* WHYY, *Philadelphia's public radio station. He is a columnist for the* Philadelphia Inquirer *and the author of four books, including* Learning from the Heart: Lessons on Living, Loving, and Listening. *Gottlieb was paralyzed from the neck down after a car accident in 1979. He has thrived despite subsequent divorce, depression, and the loss of his wife, sister, and parents.*

How long does mourning take? The answer is different for every person and every situation, but one thing is universal: it takes longer than we want it to take, and it leaves on its own time. I know from experience.

About ten years after my accident my sister died of cancer. Around the same time my wife left our marriage. I was pretty despairing, and to make matters worse my nurse noticed I had developed a bedsore. This is pretty common for people who sit in wheelchairs all day, like me. When the doctor examined the sore he told me I would have to stay in bed for thirty days! He explained that wounds to the skin heal at a rate of 1 mm a day if the environment is healthy. The doctor then gave me a patch to cover the wound, which surprised me as I knew that wounds require oxygen to heal. "Yes," he said, "wounds do need oxygen to heal. But the oxygen your wound needs is in your blood and not in the air. Every thing your wound needs to heal is already inside your body."

And so, too, with a broken heart. If the environment is healthy, everything we need to heal is already inside us. We just have to gain access to all those healing elements.

So what constitutes a healing environment?

TIME

This is the most important gift we can give ourselves. Just as getting back into my wheelchair before my wound was completely healed would have led to a setback, rushing through grief ultimately makes it worse.

TOLERANCE

Critical self judgment contaminates the healing process. Try to see yourself as a person who is suffering rather than someone who is doing something wrong. Allow yourself to feel everything you need to feel. Pain, despair, anger, confusion, and hopelessness are all emotions that wash through us and can help cleanse the wound. These emotions need not be feared, suppressed, ignored, or medicated away.

FAITH

Believe in the resilience of your own spirit. While our heads are consumed by thought, slowly but surely our hearts are beginning to heal. Just like any other wound, over time the bleeding stops and scar tissue begins to form.

A COMPASSIONATE ENVIRONMENT

Surround yourself with people who love you enough to offer you company, understanding, and a caring ear. Avoid people who offer you unsolicited advice; that's their anxiety talking and it's rarely helpful.

LOVE

Ultimately, the source of our pain is the loss of someone we love; the deeper the love, the greater the pain. But love is also the great nutrient in our healing process. Love heals whether it's being received or given. The more we are loved, the safer we feel, and the more we allow ourselves to love others, the faster we heal.

My seven-year-old grandson Sam knows all about the intertwining of grief and love. Last summer he approached me with a question that had been troubling him for a while: "Pop, how old will I be when you die?" I told him I didn't know, and when I asked him what he thought would happen to me after I died, he described his own version of heaven. He said he was afraid of my dying because he would miss me so badly. "Well, Sam," I wondered, "do you believe that I will still love you if I am in heaven?" Sam thought for a minute and said, "Sure." And he said he would still love me, too. Then I asked if he would be able to feel me loving him after I was gone. He took a few moments before he said that he thought he would always be able to feel my love for him.

As Sam now realizes, the end of a life doesn't have to mean the end of love.

–56–

MAKE A WINNING FIRST IMPRESSION

NEIL STRAUSS

> Neil Strauss, a.k.a. Style, is the world's most legendary pickup artist. He is the author of six books, including the New York Times *bestseller* The Game: Penetrating the Secret Society of Pickup Artists *and* Rules of the Game. Strauss is a contributing editor at Rolling Stone.

To make a winning impression, you must radiate a positive energy and an intriguing vibe. Because people primarily seek out and associate with those who appear to possess higher social status, you must begin by establishing your own high status. Fortunately, status is not signaled solely by wealth, fame, or beauty, but also by behavior. Here's how to build yours quickly:

- Be well groomed and comfortable in your clothing. Don't leave the house feeling self-conscious or in disarray.

- Make a grand entrance. Smile and laugh as you enter. If you're with other people, let it be seen that they're enjoying your company. If you're alone, interact with people immediately, as if you know them.

• Body language is key. Don't clutch your phone, search your purse, or fiddle with your straw. Smile, hold your head up, and maintain good posture. Stand in the center of the room—don't shrink into a corner. Make large, smooth gestures, and be neither too stiff nor too spastic.

• Lock eyes momentarily with the person you're interested in meeting, acknowledge her with a brief conspiratorial smile, and return to your conversation.

Once you've established yourself as the social center of the room, or at least a fun, magnetic person whom anyone would be lucky to meet, approach the object of your attention with the following in mind:

• People want to extricate themselves from strangers who monopolize their time. You don't want to be that stranger. So when engaging a person for the first time, convey a willingness to leave by mentioning that you must return to your friends in a moment.

• If the person is standing with others, approach with an equal or slightly higher energy level than the group; if you bring them down, they'll want to get rid of you.

• If the person is with friends, shower the friends with equal or greater attention. If you win them over, you'll win over the person you care about impressing.

• Act like a social equal, even if you're not. If the person walks by while you are engaged in another conversation, stop him, tell your friend to "hang on for a minute," and introduce yourself. Afterward, with a confident smile, say, "That's it. I didn't want to miss out. You may walk on now." Chances are no one's approached the person like this before and he will be receptive when the conversation is reinitiated.

- Avoid generic questions such as "Where are you from?" Have a couple of fun topics cued up that have nothing to do with the person, the environment, or your accomplishments. Ask for help thinking of a name for a three-legged cat, or say that your friend's girlfriend chats with guys on the Internet and you're having a debate over whether that's considered cheating. Real conundrums are preferable to made-up ones.

- Until the person warms up to you, don't give her your full attention and positive body language. While focused on the conversation, keep some distance and stand perpendicular to her, speaking over your shoulder. Create the impression that you have other things to do, and you're just stopping by to share some positive energy.

- Never be negative. Embody a world others want to be part of by appearing healthy and happy.

- Never boast. If there's something you want the person to know about you, have a friend enter the conversation and convey the information.

- Be an authority over the person's world. Teach her something new about herself, such as what her body language communicates, or appreciate something about her that others don't notice. Let her know she has met your standards, and help her feel good about herself.

- Don't appear to want anything. Figure out what the person needs (attention, approval, excitement, intimacy, enlightenment), and demonstrate that you can provide it. But don't give it away instantly—make him work for it. After you get what you want (whether a phone number, recognition, or information), stick around for a minute and talk about another subject so the person doesn't feel used.

If you successfully manage all this, you'll become a captivating person whom others want to see again—and there's no more winning impression than that.

57–

FIND A SPOUSE

JANIS SPINDEL

Janis Spindel is the founder of New York–based Janis Spindel Serious Matchmaking, Inc. She is the author of three books, including Get Serious About Getting Married. *Spindel is responsible for more than eight hundred marriages.*

I assure you that you can find a spouse quickly if you are:

1. Realistic
2. Focused
3. Willing to explore all options

When men and women truly get serious about getting married to the right person, they can make it happen fast. There is no reason for it to take a long time to hook up with Mr. or Ms. Right. When it is right it should happen swiftly, especially if you are of a certain age (thirties and forties) and have been in the adult dating world for ten to fifteen years. There is absolutely no need to date someone for a year to determine whether he or she is "the one." You should know what you want, and when you find him or her it should be obvious that you have found the right person.

My five-point plan will guide you in your search. I've seen it work more than two thousand times in my twenty-year career as a professional matchmaker. Think of yourself as being on a mission—devote time, care, and thought to it—just as you would if you were up for a promotion, changing careers, or training for a marathon. Looking for a spouse is no different—but it is more important!

1. ASSESS YOURSELF

Look in the mirror. Do you look your best? Are you healthy and fit? Are your grooming and style up to par and up to date? If you doubt yourself, hire an image consultant. Looks *do* count. The truth can be tough. Only if you look and feel your best can you compete in the relationship market and attract the kind of person you want.

2. GET REAL

What are your expectations for a mate? Do they align with your lifestyle and the kind of person you are? Make a list of the qualities you want in another person—be honest about what you are looking for and who you think will be attracted to you. You will never *find* who you are looking for if you don't *know* who you are looking for!

3. BE FRIENDLY

Make sure your attitude and body language read "marriage material"—be approachable, open, and friendly. Say hello to members of the opposite sex. Be comfortable and confident in your skin and exude cheer and happiness. Put yourself in "single" situations and not in "couple" or "friend" situations. Network!

4. BE PROACTIVE

Speaking of networking, use every option available to you. Sign up for Internet dating sites (but don't expect miracles; some people have success, others don't, and it's just one avenue to explore). Attend singles events like speed-dating nights, singles dinners and cocktail parties, and other similar gatherings—every city and town has them. Hire a matchmaker—meet with her and check her references beforehand.

5. DON'T WASTE TIME ON DEAD-END RELATIONSHIPS

Don't continue to date someone who is not marriage-minded or stay in a dead-end relationship just because it is comfortable. Let your intentions be known without seeming desperate and get out if you see the red flag or the handwriting on the wall—i.e., if he is not interested in a committed relationship, if he has a serious issue with money or work, or if your "gut" is telling you he is not the right person for you. Trust your instincts. Go back to step 2; does the person fulfill your criteria? If you are dating a person who is not marriage minded, you could be waiting a long time to walk down the aisle. Go ahead and put a time frame on it—in three months you should know if he or she is a keeper and, if so, you should be having a conversation with your partner. It should start like this: "We both have the same values, so where are we going from here. . . ?"

Finally, when you do pop the question—or answer yes to it—your engagement should not last more than six months (that's plenty of time to plan a fabulous wedding). Why wait? Complete your mission and get on with your life together!

-58-

SWEEP SOMEONE OFF THEIR FEET

PEPPER SCHWARTZ

> *Dr. Pepper Schwartz is a professor of sociology at the
> University of Washington and the relationship expert for
> Perfectmatch.com. She is the author of fourteen books,
> including* Prime: Adventures and Advice on Sex, Love,
> and the Sensual Years.

Like most people in a hurry, you may want to find love ASAP . . .
and you can. But you'll need to start out right by doing some
research first. Google the object of your desire and check out
websites that contain information regarding her background,
interests, and passions. Talk face-to-face; you don't want to look
like you are conducting an interview, but you'll need information
about values and future goals in order to strike an empathetic
cord—and avoid suggesting dinner at a steakhouse to a member of
Freedom for Animals.

Once you've gathered the information necessary to tailor your plan, implement the following steps to sweep your future mate right off her feet:

1. Demonstrate thoughtfulness. Ask a question, and act on the answer in a manner that shows you care. If she loves freesias, show up with them on your first date. If he mentioned the beach, give him a scented candle that smells like an island. Only small gifts are appropriate; extravagance will reek of desperation.

2. The first date: if you are a man, stay traditional but aim high. Secure the hard-to-get restaurant reservation; purchase center-court seats; arrange a boat ride to a special place. Plan something thoughtful based on what you have discovered through your research; if you are both runners, suggest taking a run together on a secret trail. If you are a woman, be a knockout. Wear something sexy but not trashy; have your hair and makeup done professionally.

3. Keep conversation light, but every now and then simply gaze at the other person with a smile. If he looks embarrassed or uncertain, say, "I just can't believe how connected to you I feel. I am intrigued in a very unusual way." Adapt this approach to your own style, but make sure to communicate your fascination and your feeling that you are in the grip of something special. Let the other person talk more than you, but show some life and come across as intelligent and well rounded.

4. At the end of the first date kiss sweetly with restraint and a touch of longing, applying just enough pressure to show you have the potential to unleash passion.

5. If you are a man, e-mail her the same night to let her know how lucky you feel to have connected with her. If you are a woman, wait until he writes to you. Some guys need to be the pursuer, and

if you make the first move he may retreat. When he does contact you, mention that wonderful kiss and how you kept running it through your head all day. Be available, but not too available. Make (or accept) another date happily, but not for the next night.

6. Second or third date: you've built anticipation through a couple of great kisses, flirtatious e-mails, and heartfelt flattering; now it's time to go all out on something romantic. Book a table at sunset along a scenic river or at a ski lodge in the mountains. It should be clear that you've spent a great deal of thought and energy planning the evening.

7. Wear a specific perfume or cologne and let the person pine for the very smell of you.

8. Communicate your desire: "I have to kiss you." "I can't believe I found you." Pour it on, but stop if your sentiments aren't immediately reciprocated.

9. Close the deal: take a moonlit walk; hold hands under the table at a jazz club. This is the moment when you look into each other's eyes and kiss—hard, passionately—and can't let go. Your evening should end in total desire and a mutual feeling that you've begun an amazing relationship.

Now that you've swept the person off her feet, you need to maintain the passion and energy. Call with a quick reminder of a special moment. Send a note about how devastatingly sexy she is. Tell him he is an unbelievable lover—or, if you aren't there yet, that he makes you hot when you see him.

I hope you want to continue to see this person because by this time he or she will have become your lapdog.

–59–

BUILD A GREAT RELATIONSHIP

ROBI LUDWIG

Dr. Robi Ludwig is a psychotherapist who appears regularly on CNN as well as the Today show. *She is the former host of TLC's reality show* One Week to Save Your Marriage. *She is the coauthor of* Till Death Do Us Part: Love, Marriage, and the Mind of the Killer Spouse *and host of GSN's* Without Prejudice.

A chieving a great relationship can feel like one of life's great unanswered mysteries, especially for those who put themselves in the romantically challenged category. But some mysteries are easier to solve than others, and how to have a great relationship is one of them. So here are the key elements to creating the relationship of your dreams—stronger and faster than ever.

MR. AND MS. RIGHT

Begin by choosing someone with good character. Choosing a partner who has questionable character is like putting all your money into a bad stock. It doesn't matter how much you put into it; at the end of the day, it's going to be a bad investment. You have to use a combination of your head and your heart when choosing a romantic relationship.

It helps to define your ideal relationship and partner. Think reality, not fantasy. Ask yourself not only what you want but what you need. Challenge yourself to come up with the things you can and can't live without in a relationship, what you require from this person on a day-to-day basis, and what you need to thrive.

THE RELATIONSHIP

Now that you have found your Mr. or Ms. Right it's time to secure your great relationship so you can move it forward.

All successful relationships are built on a feeling of mutual respect. It's important to show your partner how much you enjoy, learn from, and appreciate him. Only speak well of your partner. How you speak about him has a powerful impact on what your relationship will ultimately look like.

It's way too easy to get caught up in a chronic fault-finding mode, but resist this all-too-natural tendency. Don't expect perfection—it doesn't exist! The way to quickly achieve a rewarding, romantic relationship is to focus on your partner's positive traits. Call her to tell her you love her, spend quality time together, and think creatively; the possibilities are endless.

When you count your blessings and focus on feeling grateful about your relationship, this feeling of goodwill can carry you through the inevitable tough times. During an argument, it's hard to appreciate your partner's stronger points. That's why it's so important to get a head start in this area. Be sensitive to your partner's needs, and be willing to forgive quickly. Remember, it's way more important to make the relationship right than to be right.

Treat your partner as though she is the most important person in the world by plugging into who she is and what's important to her. Ask questions and communicate regularly. This is the best way to establish a common understanding as well as to come to terms with your inevitable differences.

People tend to end up with partners who feel familiar to them. One way to foster this special feeling of familiarity is to create a unique history together. Celebrating and enjoying unique moments in a relationship creates a sense of intimacy as well as strengthens a couple's emotional bond and sense of satisfaction with each other.

Finally, leave some space to miss each other. Members of couples need to maintain their own sense of individuality. Remember the importance of taking care of yourself and pursuing a life that feels rewarding, passionate, and fulfilling. Your partner can't fulfill all of your needs and isn't meant to. So be good to yourself, be kind to your partner, and remember that we all are works in progress.

–60–

PLAN A WEDDING

TORY L. COOPER

*Tory L. Cooper is a wedding and event planner based in
Las Vegas, the wedding capital of the world.
She was named "Best Wedding Planner" by
Las Vegas Life magazine.*

A short engagement is one way to eliminate the undue stress that often results from a long wait between "I will" and "I do," but it can't help you escape the details. The easiest thing you can do to plan your wedding faster without missing a beat is to hire a professional wedding planner—the musical conductor to your orchestra. Planners can execute a wedding to meet your schedule, whether it's in twenty-four hours or four months. But whether you hire a planner or not, organization is critical when speedy planning is a priority, so here are the things to think about:

1. LOCATION! LOCATION! LOCATION!

The location will set the tone for your entire wedding celebration. If you are in a rush, be flexible about the date, as availability of

your preferred location may be limited. Think outside the box—
a Sunday or Friday night wedding can be just as fun as one on a
Saturday night, which typically gets booked far in advance. If you
have your heart set on a destination wedding, make sure to choose
a location that guests can fly in and out of easily. Last-minute travel
plans are often tougher to arrange, so destinations with direct
flights help you and your guests avoid unnecessary problems.

2. SET A BUDGET

List wedding elements in order of priority. Rings, bride's and
groom's attire, venue, food and beverage, wedding cake, invitations, flowers, linen and decor, music, photography and videogra-
phy, hair and makeup, officiant, party favors, transportation—each
is important, but you must decide where to allocate your precious
resources. This will help you avoid some difficult decisions that
are sure to come up in the planning process. Decide who will be
paying for what in advance. Having a short engagement may mean
you can cut back on your guest list, which helps keep your budget
in check.

3. SELECT YOUR WEDDING VENDORS

Most planners and caterers have a preferred vendor list. Using
these vendors will help you avoid months of research. Save time
by contacting vendors by phone or online rather than in-person
visits. View photos of their work on websites and interview them
over the phone to ensure that your personalities are a match. If
you are concerned about not meeting the vendors in person, check
references for added insurance. When you select your vendors,
immediately ask for agreements to be drawn up—you should be
able to obtain contracts within forty-eight hours.

4. PURCHASE YOUR WEDDING DRESS OR TUXEDO

To ensure a quicker turnaround, make sure the wedding and tuxedo shops you use have alteration experts on-site. Your tuxedo store should offer to deliver once the tuxedo has been altered. Select your bridal party's attire only after selecting your own. By purchasing bridesmaids' attire off the rack at a wedding dress store or a department store, you can have your dresses overnight. Even better, delegate this task to your bridesmaids by picking a color scheme and asking them to choose their own dresses in that hue.

5. FINALIZE THE CEREMONY AND RECEPTION FLOW

Meet with the person performing the ceremony to assure the service reflects your personality. Just because you are crunched for time doesn't mean you have to forego personalizing your ceremony.

In a single meeting try to finalize as many elements as possible: confirm the menu with a tasting from the caterer; view a sample table arranged with your centerpiece, linen, and decor; select your music, including first dance; and reconfirm the time line and all details. Always follow your instincts. By doing so, you will not prolong decisions that can be made quickly.

6. OBTAIN YOUR MARRIAGE LICENSE

Easily overlooked and often forgotten, a marriage license is necessary to legalize your bond, so don't forget this step amid all the other preparations. Go to the county courthouse in the city of your wedding ceremony. Generally, you will be asked for proof of ID, your mother's maiden name, and a small fee for the license, so be prepared. A marriage license is valid for one year, so if you can get it sooner rather than later, it is one more item you can check off your list.

-61-

WRITE THANK-YOU NOTES

CAROLYNE ROEHM

Carolyne Roehm is the author of nine books, including
A Passion for Parties. *She is the editor of* CR Style, *her
bimonthly online magazine. The late fashion designer Bill
Blass called her "the ultimate tastemaker."*

Get ready, get set . . . write.

There is nothing lovelier than receiving a thoughtful thank-you note from your guests or sending one after receiving a gift. For years I have saved meaningful thank-you notes, which act as a journal of special events in my life. In this fast-paced, stressful world, gestures such as a beautifully written note are even more appreciated.

PREPARE

The key to having the discipline to write notes and letters is ready access to all the necessary supplies. Designating one cabinet, drawer, or box that holds everything lets you begin the task with half the work already done. Always keep the following items in your supply cabinet:

- Address book
- Stamps
- Fountain pens
- Inks
- Colored felt-tip pens (choose whatever you like to write with)
- Personalized papers, including note cards, correspondence cards, and business cards
- Letterhead

I also keep on hand my personal stationery, in several colors and with a variety of monograms, to cover the range of formal and informal notes required for different occasions; an assortment of nonpersonalized cards and stationery; and a selection of birthday and get-well cards, invitations, reminders, and place cards.

Have a stamp made of your monogram; this is a great time-saver. I had mine made in several sizes to fit various gift-card inserts and note cards. If I need to send a small orchid plant to a hostess as a special thank-you, a stamped gift card with a ribbon tie is the perfect finish.

Before you start writing, decide whether you will be sending a handwritten or an e-mail note. Here is my rule of thumb:

- Handwritten or engraved invitations require a handwritten note.
- A gift received requires a handwritten note.
- A special occasion—for example, my girlfriend hosting a birth-

day lunch for me—requires a handwritten note and may also require a small gift such as flowers, a book, or a CD.

• E-mail invitations can be handled with e-mail responses.

One final preparatory tip: If you plan to send a small thank-you gift, preorder it and send the thank-you card to the merchant before delivery.

WRITE

The most effective notes are ones written by those who are observant and good listeners. If someone has taken great pride in preparing a meal, setting a table, creating a floral arrangement, or selecting special music, you should acknowledge this in your thank-you note. My secret for remembering the highlights of an event is to always keep a jotter and pen in my purse, or, if you prefer, keep a note pad and pen next to your bed and jot down a few quick observations from the evening before you go to sleep. This ensures that you will remember important details the next morning.

When writing a thank-you note, always start by thanking the host for the invitation. The key to a good thank-you note is to include a highlight of the event. In the order of the evening, reference a memory from one or more of the following:

• Cocktails

• Conversation with other guests; meeting children or other family members

• Table setting

• Flowers or music

• Menu

• Home, particularly if decorated for the holidays

The more personalized and specific you are, the more thoughtful and well written your note will be.

When sending a thank-you note for a gift, acknowledge the gift and mention how you plan to put it to good use. If I receive a new CD I will tell the sender that it is being downloaded to my iPod as I'm writing the note and I will be enjoying it during my next morning workout. I will also acknowledge the band and thank the sender for introducing me to new talent.

The most important thing to remember, however, is to send some sort of acknowledgment promptly. If you forget to do so, explain that life is currently moving faster than your memory, and apologize for the late acknowledgment. All of us can understand that situation.

On a final note, encourage children to write thank-you notes for invitations and presents. The sooner they can get in the habit of saying thank you in writing or in person, the better. Saying thank you should never be perceived as a chore.

–62–

GET PREGNANT

LISA MASTERSON

Dr. Lisa Masterson is a Santa Monica–based gynecologist, obstetrician, and fertility specialist. She is a cast member of the medical team featured on the nationally syndicated series The Doctors.

With more and more women delaying childbirth and having babies after the age of thirty-five, the percentage of women experiencing problems with fertility has significantly increased. If you're hoping to become pregnant, having healthy and knowing your body are essential for maintaining and improving fertility. Below are some research-proven tips to increase your chances of getting pregnant—now:

- KNOW YOUR CYCLE. A woman's regular period is an indication that she is ovulating every month. Knowing when ovulation will occur—when the egg will leave the ovary to await "sperm charming" in the tube—is a great help in getting pregnant. You can confirm your ovulation at home by using over-the-counter kits or at your doctor's office with a blood test. Consult your physician if you are experiencing irregular periods or periods that come more often or less frequently than normal (every twenty-one to thirty-five days).

- AN OUNCE OF PREVENTION GOES A LONG WAY. Sexually transmitted diseases (STDs) can decrease your fertility even if you are not experiencing symptoms. Protect yourself from STDs by limiting your number of sexual partners and using condoms. Also, get annual STD screenings, as early treatment can help preserve the health of your uterus, tubes, and ovaries.

- EAT HEALTHY FOR TWO. Eating carbohydrates that take longer to digest—like whole grains, beans, fresh fruits, and vegetables—can improve your chances of pregnancy by facilitating ovulation.

- ALL FATS ARE NOT CREATED EQUAL. You should avoid trans fats, but unsaturated fats, like avocado, peanuts, almonds, tuna, Cheddar cheese, and salmon, have been shown to improve fertility by stimulating hormone production, increasing insulin sensitivity, and decreasing inflammation. Eating more protein from plants and less protein from animals can also help to improve ovulation and thus fertility.

- GOT WHOLE MILK? One or two daily servings of whole milk or whole milk products—such as full-fat yogurt or cottage cheese—may help to improve fertility.

- MAINTAIN YOUR HEALTHY WEIGHT. When you are trying to get pregnant, you should neither starve yourself nor overeat. Being overweight or underweight will decrease your fertility by altering your normal menstrual cycle and interrupting ovulation. Women who have a body mass index (BMI) between 20 and 24 are least likely to experience problems with infertility.

- GET YOUR HEART GOING. Aerobic exercise not only helps you maintain your healthy weight but also directly improves your fertility. Exercise increases muscle health and keeps metabolic systems working well to prevent imbalances that can interrupt ovulation. In general, most women should exercise thirty minutes every day. The recommended length of exercise may vary if you are underweight or overweight.

- KEEP TIME ON YOUR SIDE. Every woman's fertility is on a time clock. As you get older the number and quality of your eggs decrease, thereby decreasing your chances of getting pregnant. If you are in your twenties and considering delaying pregnancy you may want to freeze your eggs. If you are thirty-five or older and experiencing fertility problems, consult your doctor right away. Even though great technological advances have been made in fertility treatment, perfection is elusive and time is still important.

- DON'T FORGET ABOUT YOUR MAN. Thirty percent of infertility cases are the result of male infertility. Encourage your partner to have regular physicals, eat healthy, and decrease or omit drug and alcohol usage, which can decrease his sperm count.

- RELAX! You need to decrease the amount of stress in your life, as study after study has established that stress decreases fertility and can be a significant obstacle to getting pregnant. This may be a good time to take that island vacation you've been thinking about.

-63-

DISCUSS A DIFFICULT ISSUE WITH YOUR SPOUSE

HARVILLE HENDRIX

Dr. Harville Hendrix is a marital therapist and author of Getting the Love You Want: A Guide for Couples, *which has appeared eleven times on the* New York Times *bestseller list and sixteen times on* The Oprah Winfrey Show *and included in her top twenty all-time shows. He and his wife, Dr. Helen Lakelly Hunt, have coauthored eight books. They are cocreators of Imago Relationship Therapy, which is practiced in thirty countries by more than two thousand therapists.*

Most conversations are parallel monologues in which two people are talking and no one is listening. The supposed listener is usually thinking about what he or she is going to say, but no one can listen and think at the same time. Listening requires you to empty your mind of the chatter of your own thoughts so you can hear the meaning in your partner's words. Both partners need to learn a new way of talking, called "couple's dialogue," but you don't have to be a couple to use it.

A couple's dialogue has three parts: mirroring, validating, and empathizing.

MIRRORING

When you mirror another person you reflect back accurately what the other is saying and you exclude your thoughts and feelings in your response. When the speaker has finished talking and has been mirrored, the listening partner should summarize all that the other person has said—again without adding anything. Since most people tend to retain only the first and last sentence, and are itching to make a comment, an accurate summary is very important. This is how mirroring looks:

Speaker talks about their issue: "You were late and did not call."

Listener mirrors: "Let me see if I got that. You said I was late and did not call. Did I get it?"

Speaker says yes or no, and if no, sends it again.

Listener continues to mirror and, when she gets it right, says: "Is there more about that?" This is very important, since most listeners tend to say unhelpfully: "Are you done yet?"

Speaker: "Yes. There is more. We agreed that if you were ever going to be late, you would call. When you didn't call I got worried that something might have happened to you. Then

I thought, We made this agreement because you are often late and don't call, and then I got angry and felt disrespected. And the dinner was cold."

Listener mirrors and asks, "Is there more?" until everything has been said and the speaker says, "There is no more."

Listener summarizes: "Since I am often late, we had an agreement that if I am ever late I would call, and I didn't. First you worried about me, and then you recalled our agreement and got angry and felt disrespected. And the dinner was cold. Did I get it all?"

Speaker responds with yes or no. If no, listener attempts summary until it is accurate and complete.

VALIDATING

In all relationships, there are always two points of view. Validating is seeing and accepting the truth in another point of view without surrendering your own. As the listener, this means you attempt to see the logic in the speaker's words. Whether we like it or not, all people make sense, even our partners! In great relationships, both points of view are always accepted and honored as the starting point and both people work from there to create a third option that includes both points of view. Validation looks like this:

Receiver: "I get it." Or, "You make sense, and the sense you are making is that . . ." The receiver repeats again what he has heard, but this time he attempts to see the logic behind the other person's thoughts, e.g., "It makes sense to me that you would feel angry and disrespected, since I did agree to be home at seven PM, and getting home late broke my agreement. Did I get that right?" You do not have to, and should not, defend yourself. Just validate your partner's experience. This helps the sender feel visible and respected, and that in itself often resolves an issue.

EMPATHIZING

When you empathize, you attempt to hear and reflect back the feelings attached to the sender's experience, whether she has expressed them overtly or not. If she has not expressed feelings, you attempt to imagine what she might be feeling. If she has expressed feelings such as tears or anger, then simply reflect that back. Do not tell her what she is feeling for two reasons: (1) that would be intrusive and mind reading; and (2) what you think she is feeling is probably what you are feeling. This is how empathy looks:

Receiver: "You feel disrespected and angry. Is that what you feel?" It is important to check to see if you got the feelings right. If he says yes, then ask: "Do you have other feelings?" If you got it wrong, then ask what he is feeling. Then mirror that back and say: "Thanks for telling me about your issue and your feelings."

Take turns. When your partner acknowledges that he feels fully heard, then ask if he will now listen to your reality and mirror, validate, and empathize with you. This levels the playing field. Conversation now takes place between equals who cocreate productive outcomes around any issue.

When you begin to learn this new way of talking, it is important to use the structure rigidly—like learning any skill. It may feel wooden and time-consuming at first, but with consistent use and no emotional debris to clean up, it will become effective and time-efficient. Using this process creates a safe emotional climate where connection deepens and grows—which is usually what most partners want anyway.

–64–

FIND A LOST CHILD IN A CROWD

CLINT VAN ZANDT

Clint Van Zandt spent twenty-five years with the FBI as a chief hostage negotiator and supervisor in the Bureau's Behavioral Science Unit—better known as the Silence of the Lambs Unit. He is widely credited with leading the team that led to the capture of the Unabomber. He is the author of Facing Down Evil: Life on the Edge as an FBI Hostage Negotiator *and an analyst for MSNBC.*

More than 70 percent of families have lost one or more children at least once. Two thousand children are reported missing on a daily basis, either in or around their home or in high population density areas like shopping malls, parks, public pools, beaches, resorts, and airports. Given the statistical likelihood that you, as a parent, grandparent, or caregiver, may need to quickly find a child who has accidentally separated himself from you, you need to have a plan in effect to ensure an efficient search.

A good precautionary measure to take before leaving the house or school is to place in each child's pocket a note including the name of the child and a cell phone number where a responsible caregiver can be immediately contacted. Don't put your home address on the note, as you do not want a stranger telling your child he must drive her home.

Before entering a public place, make sure everyone knows the plan and where they should go should they become separated. Families should always have a prearranged meeting place—the fountain area in a large outdoor mall or the pharmacy in a grocery store. Be sure your child understands that under no circumstances should she leave the last area where she saw you, except to go to the prearranged meeting place. She should tell a police officer, a store manager, or a woman with children that she is lost. She should not sit alone and look lost, as such behavior can attract predators.

Cell phones can help aid in a search by tracking the *ping* the phone makes off the closest cell phone tower, so it's a great idea to provide children with their own phones if possible. In addition, when going to a crowded place like an arena or an amusement park, use your phone's camera (if it has one) to take a picture of each child in your group. This will provide you with an immediate record of the physical and clothing description of each child, one that can be shared with searchers and even downloaded, copied, and distributed as needed.

Dress children in brightly colored clothing—particularly yellow and green—a strong visual search aid should they become separated. As it is difficult for young children to see the face of every adult towering over them in a crowd, consider carrying a large handkerchief or scarf that you can tie just under your knee should they become lost—this item will give the child a visual point of reference that he can readily see from his own vantage point.

Should a member of your group become separated, immediately notify local security about the missing person. Most malls, amusement parks, and other public parks have emergency procedures they will enact, such as paging the missing child and sealing all points of exit, to ensure that your child neither wanders out of the location alone nor is removed under duress by an abductor. Security will promptly notify all store or facility employees of the missing person and will institute a review of all security-camera footage. While searching on your own, stand on a bench to elevate yourself high above the crowd, and narrow your search by looking for the color of clothing that your child is wearing.

Last, when your child is found, be quick to praise and not berate him. You want your child to understand how much you missed him and that you should stay closer together in the future. If you scold your child, you will be adding guilt to the already terrifying experience he just went through.

–65–

TEACH A DOG TO SIT

TAMAR GELLER

Tamar Geller is the resident dog expert on NBC's the Today show and the founder of The Loved Dog, a cage-free day-care and boarding center for dogs in Los Angeles. She is the author of The Loved Dog: The Playful Nonaggressive Way to Teach Your Dog Good Behavior *and creator of a DVD,* Celebrate Your Dog! The Loved Dog Way of Training.

Just as you choose your path in life, you have a choice of what path to take when it comes to raising your dog: the positive way or the negative way. What kind of leader do you want to be: a tough dictator like Saddam Hussein, or a benevolent leader such as Martin Luther King, Jr.?

Your approach to training, or, to use my preferred term, "coaching," a dog, should be based on love and respect rather than on fear. The dog and the owner should enjoy the ongoing relationship and celebrate each other.

What makes a dog behave in a certain way? What is the force that drives a dog's behavior? The force is whatever the dog associates with pain and with pleasure. He'll do anything to avoid pain and gain pleasure. Therefore, the first thing a dog should learn is something that will make him feel successful, and therefore give him a sense of pleasure. Learning to sit is the best skill to begin with.

I don't believe in using a leash to teach dogs new behavior, and we will never push the dog's behind to the floor.

THE MAGNET

Hold a yummy treat in your hand and cover it with your fingers. Put it by the dog's nose and move it a few inches to the right and then a few inches to the left. If the dog is following you with his hand, you have a "magnet."

Bring the "magnet" to your dog's nose and move it back over his head slightly toward his tail. The dog will follow you and will look up at you. The ideal treat height is one inch above his head. Don't put the treat too high or he will jump to try to get it. Because of the way a dog is built, as he looks up, he will sit down. At that moment you want to release the treat into his mouth and happily say, "S-i-i-i-i-i-i-t!"

CHANGE YOUR OWN BODY POSITION

Most people coach their dog while they are standing up. Then when they are lying down and relaxing, the dog does not listen to them. That is because the dog learned to associate being coached only with its owner standing up. Because children are shorter than adults, it is important to bend down or sit on the floor and make sure that you coach your dog on how to sit using the "magnet" while you are in both reclining and sitting positions. This will insure that "Sit" works in multiple positions, so that your child will be able to coach your dog effectively as well.

CHANGE YOUR LOCATION

You also want to practice that newfound knowledge in as many rooms as possible around your house, at friends' homes, and on the street. One of the best places to practice is by your front door.

RELEVANCE TRAINING

Now that he associates his good behavior with the rewards, your dog should be doing things not just because you say so but because he wants to comply. We start by using treats as the "magnet," but within two days of consistent training, we must stop giving treats for every "Sit." Instead, you want to incorporate sitting into the dog's daily routine. Teach him to sit for everything the way you would teach a child to say "Please" when asking for anything. Before you put your dog's food down, ask him to sit. Before you give him a toy, before you invite him on your bed, before you put his leash on, and before you open the door to go for a walk, ask him to sit. Do it before you let him into the car and before you let him out. You get the drift. Getting those things will become the reward and there will be no need for treats anymore.

Celebrate your dog and have fun coaching!

PLEASURE

—66—

GET IN A GOOD MOOD

DAN BAKER

Dr. Dan Baker is a medical psychologist. He was one of the original developers of Canyon Ranch spas and founded their award-winning Life Enhancement Program. Dr. Baker has devoted his life to teaching people how to be happy and is the author of three books, including What Happy People Know: How the New Science of Happiness Can Change Your Life for the Better.

Did you wake up this morning hoping to have a lousy day? Of course not, but sometimes you end up in a bad mood anyway. People experience a spectrum of moods, and it's okay to give in to a dark one.

The trick is to not stay in a bad mood for too long or you'll become depressed, as bad moods tend to narrow focus. "Target Acquisition Fixation" is a phenomenon seen in the training of fighter pilots, who can become so focused on their target that everything else around them disappears—similar to when you look at the screen of your computer for too long and lose your peripheral vision. This phenomenon extends to the realm of moods; for example, when you are in such a state of malaise that you lose the ability to see the goodness around you.

In such times, it often seems that breaking free of your funk is simply not possible; but there are ways to get to a better place. Here's how:

LIVE WITH PURPOSE

You need to know what resonates with you most meaningfully, for it is these things that will reliably put you in a good mood. For example, you may love your work and the mission of your employer, and feel that you contribute to its success. Or perhaps you love helping your children with their homework or working in a soup kitchen. If you can't articulate clearly in a few words your sense of purpose, make it your mission to discover that purpose.

PREPARE YOUR MIND

Humans think habitually (e.g., if you are asked your favorite color you will usually respond the same way without much thought). So you need to build the neurological pathways that orient your perspective toward what is good in your life. Prepare your mind by performing the following mental exercise six times a day: Ask yourself what you see in your immediate environment that makes you smile. Then allow yourself the time to think about each thing.

CONTEMPLATE THE GOOD THINGS IN LIFE

I moved from a Sun Belt state to the Midwest last year. If I look outside and see it is rainy and cold and say, "I hate this weather," I will start feeling really down. Instead, I think to myself, "Wow, weather is a pretty amazing thing. I'm in a warm home. I have a fireplace and I am grateful for that." You can't do this all the time, but most of the things you trouble yourself over don't amount to much in the long run.

PREPARE YOUR ENVIRONMENT

Truly happy people are participants in shaping their own destiny. One of the greatest influences on mood is environment, so be proactive when creating yours by preparing your surroundings to optimize their good-mood-generating potential. Create a harmonious family environment and fill it with art you love, your favorite flowers, and inspiring table books. Give your work space a sense of personality and keep your best friends' numbers easily accessible.

CHANGE YOUR PERSPECTIVE

When you are in a bad mood, do something that helps you engage the world in a more positive light:

- Hold a baby
- Call your best friend
  Write a thank-you note you've been putting off
- Prepare your favorite food
- Go to your favorite restaurant
- Take a walk in a lively area or beautiful place

LEARN FROM HAPPY PEOPLE

Happy people share certain common traits, and if you follow their lead you'll tend to live your life in a blissful state, too:

- They have a sense of personal responsibility and not a sense of entitlement.

- They have a can-do attitude.
- They are persistent and actively find a way to get to a better emotional place.
- They don't feel victimized, but rather manage life crises in a positive manner.
- They learn from life experiences—even the most painful ones, which often offer the most profound lessons.
- They celebrate positive events.

Ultimately, if your mood is adversely affecting your relationships, health, and, most important, your general daily function, it is time to see a professional. If you have struggled intermittently in the past with depression, seek help if your current state of melancholy has lasted for two weeks or longer. If this is the first time you have experienced depressive episodes, wait no longer than a month or two before seeking help. It is essential that you not let a depressed frame of mind prevail for too long, because the sooner it is treated, the more likely it is to be resolved.

–67–

MAKE SOMEONE FEEL GOOD

EDWIN TRINKA

Edwin Trinka has been a doorman at
New York's legendary Plaza Hotel for more than
forty-two years.

As a doorman at a luxury hotel, one of the most important elements of my job is to make people feel welcome as soon as they exit their car or step up to the door. Over the years, I have discovered that the most effective way to make people feel good is to make them feel optimistic and at ease. If you can do that, they'll be your friends for life. Here's how I do it:

SMILE

The first person to meet a guest at the front door of our hotel is me, the doorman. And a bright smile starts everyone off in the right direction. With a positive attitude, all parties are immediately put at ease and are able to communicate effectively.

SAY "PLEASE" AND "THANK YOU"

As a child, teachers and parents always tried to instill in us those magic words, *please* and *thank you*. To this day they are fundamental to our society. They are so simple to offer yet have so much to do with how you are perceived. People judge you by the manner in which you speak to them, and no matter how many times you hear these words, their universally warming effect is never blunted. Of course, I say "please" and "thank you" over and over as a doorman. When I hail a cab for a guest I thank him for letting me be of service and thank the driver for picking him up. Many drivers return and thank me for that. It's a wonderful feeling.

BE APPROACHABLE

When I begin my day clean-shaven, with shiny shoes and uniform pressed, it makes me seem approachable. And when people perceive you as approachable, they immediately feel more confident about themselves.

HAVE A SENSE OF HUMOR

A good sense of humor can quickly change frowns into laughter. If you change the way you look at things, the things you look at change. I remember one time, outside the hotel, a taxi came too close to the curb and slightly brushed a young newlywed's bag. At first the guest was a wreck, but then she said to her husband that she'll always remember her first day of her married life when she recalls this incident. Those newlyweds now return for their anniversary every year, always sharing a laugh about the cab that came too close.

GO ABOVE AND BEYOND

As a professional doorman I strive to do more than the ordinary. Take the same approach with old friends and new acquaintances and you'll be remembered warmly forever. One very early morning I had a guest who needed his shoes shined for an important meeting, and no place was open. Thinking fast, I ran into the locker room, took out my shoeshine kit from my locker, and proceeded to shine his shoes. He went to his meeting, got his promotion, and, needless to say, we have been friends ever since.

Try some of my daily tips and you'll see not only a change in how others feel in your presence, but also in how you feel. It is hard to have a bad day when you are making other people feel good.

-68-

MAKE FRIENDS

SALLY HORCHOW
AND ROGER HORCHOW

Sally and Roger Horchow are the father/daughter coauthors of The Art of Friendship: 70 Simple Rules for Making Meaningful Connections.

Anyone who's ever experienced the thrill of having a "new best friend" has probably also seen that fast and furious friendship crash and burn, like a brief, torrid love affair without a courtship period. But making fast friends and making friends faster can also mean making friends that last. (Now say that ten times fast!) Here's how:

1. MAKE ROOM FOR NEW FRIENDS

Contrary to popular belief, one's friend "real estate" is not finite. It's possible to clear space in your life for new friendships without sacrificing existing ones. Start by banishing those old rote excuses, like "My plate's too full," or "I hardly have time for my regular friends," or "I don't have the energy."

2. CHANGE YOUR HABITS

Hastening the search may require straying from your daily path (literally, as in walking a new way to work or trying a different coffee shop) or making a real effort to place yourself in friend-friendly situations. Join a group of people who do an activity you like to do (Tennis, anyone? Cooking club? Friends of the Alamo?). Let yourself be "set up," take a group trip, or host or attend a party when you might normally opt for a night with your TiVo.

3. HONE YOUR "FRIENDSHIP ANTENNA"

Be on DEFCON 5/High Alert for friends at all times. Learn to look for and evaluate clues about your potential friend, using your "friendship antenna": Is he reading a book you like? Does she seem affable and open to conversation? Is she saying or doing something that you can observe before making your move? (Subtle eavesdropping is encouraged—you might pick up on a great conversation "in"—or a horrifying clue that could help you avoid the person altogether.)

4. USE SMALL TALK STRATEGICALLY

Small talk. Gotta love it, can't hate it. "How are you?" "Strange weather we're having," "How 'bout those Mets," and all of their beloved brother banalities are not going away anytime soon. But you can also use small talk as a way to tread into deeper waters, further evaluate a friend candidate, and get to know someone. Use a topical "pickup line" or a specific question to put people at ease. Compliments ("Great scarf!") or self-deprecating remarks ("I never know how to dress for these things") will jump-start any conversation.

5. BE PROACTIVE

Once you've zeroed in on your new potential friend and laid the friend groundwork   having shared a laugh or discovered a mutual interest—make sure you follow through. In the dating world, this would be called "getting digits." (Well, okay: you should "get digits" here, too—or an e-mail address.) The point is: let the person know you'd like to see him or her again and don't leave without knowing how to do so.

6. DON'T DROP THE BALL

Follow up. Use whatever means you were given (don't show up on her doorstep if she gave you her e-mail) and get back in touch. Unlike dating, there are no three-day delay rules here, so if you call the next day or don't get around to it for a week, it's no big deal. Remind the person of when you met, spark a memory of the funny joke or interesting conversation topic you shared, and make a plan to get together *in person*—e-mail exchanges are great for building a rapport, but a real friendship cannot ignite without in-person contact.

7. PEEL BACK THE ONION

To cut to the chase and let the real friendship begin, make your conversations count. Take every advantage to get to know your friend better. Peel back the first, superficial layers to get to the more meaningful conversations. Listen. And make the fast friendship last!

−69−

PLAN A DINNER PARTY

COLIN COWIE

Colin Cowie is an event planner whose celebrity clientele includes Oprah Winfrey, Tom Cruise, and Jerry Seinfeld. He is a lifestyle contributor for the CBS Early Show *and the author of seven books, including* Colin Cowie Chic: The Guide to Life As It Should Be.

The key to planning a successful dinner party quickly is to be resourceful and organized. So, instead of being chained to the kitchen stove while your friends are enjoying themselves in the other room, plan ahead. You want to have as much fun as your guests, and if you're the head chef, bottle washer, and waiter, chances are you won't be having all that much fun.

To get started, here are the basics:

THE FOOD AND DRINK

Determine what you can realistically prepare without too much stress. Choose a foolproof menu, which means avoiding soufflés and other dishes that will get ruined if you're fifteen minutes off schedule (whether because your guests are enjoying themselves over cocktails or someone is late). Savory stews, soups, and casseroles can be prepared (at least in part) ahead of time and served easily, and will allow you to sit and dine with your guests.

A telephone and great takeout can be your best ally. If you love to bake and can't imagine yourself doing anything more, find a favorite restaurant and order in. If at all possible, drop your serving platters off that morning so the food is ready to serve when you bring it home. At the very least, remove the food from the takeout cartons and serve it on your own platters. Make the first course simple but spectacular. Choose dishes that are visual as well as delicious—those that balance color, temperature, texture, and taste.

I always offer a sexy and potent cocktail to jump-start the party. You can premix a pitcher so it's ready to pour and set it on a tray for guests to help themselves. Be sure to have your glassware, garnishes (olives, lemon slices), and ice ready for the taking.

THE PREPARATION

Stay organized. Labeling plates and serving dishes for each course with Post-it notes will help you avoid last-minute confusion. Be sure to clean and polish your serving pieces a day or two before the party, and aim to have the table set in advance and all your slicing, dicing, washing, and peeling done several hours before guests arrive.

Map out the timing—it's the key to a successful party and one ingredient that doesn't cost a dime but is so often overlooked. Schedule when guests will arrive, when the cocktail hour will start, and when dinner will be served. Forty-five minutes to an hour is perfect for cocktails before dinner. Don't let certain parts of the evening drag along only to find yourself rushing others.

Set a deadline of an hour before the party to get everything ready. Use the twenty minutes before your guests arrive to put out ice, add any finishing touches to the table, and set out the appetizers. Light the candles, adjust the lights, turn on the music, open the wine, pour yourself a cocktail, and take a few moments to glance over the room and make sure everything is in place.

THE GUESTS

Create an interesting guest list. Try to mix groups of friends and introduce new people to one another. Place cards are a must for parties of more than eight guests; they prevent confusion when it comes time to sit down and allow you to balance the energy and dynamics of the table. Don't put the Chatty Cathys at one end and shrinking violets at the other. Separating spouses also makes for more free and lively conversation.

THE ATMOSPHERE

Music is the ultimate mood maker. If you don't have an iPod with some fun and dynamic playlists, program a variety of CD's for random play so you'll have continuous music throughout the night. You'll want something lively and upbeat like lounge music for the cocktail hour to help conversation along, and something more subdued and instrumental during dinner. Keep the music playing from the moment guests arrive until the door closes behind them.

I'm a self-diagnosed ambiance junkie. So dim the lights, burn some fragrant candles, and buy a few fresh flowers on your way home from work. Sight, smell, sound, and touch are just as important as taste when it comes to entertaining.

POLITELY EXIT A CONVERSATION

JULEANNA GLOVER

Juleanna Glover is a lobbyist and a founding principal of The Ashcroft Group in Washington, D.C. She is known as the premier Washington hostess—bringing together renowned Democrats and Republicans alike into her home.

At social events of any kind—formal or informal, big or small, work or leisure—it is easy to get stuck in awkward conversations filled with stilted exchanges and painful silence. In these electric times, our minds race for a means of escape. The old standby exit line is "I'm going to grab a glass of wine—can I get you anything?" But what if the bar is right in front of you, or, worse yet, your glass is still full? And what if you just don't want to be that obvious? Everyone knows the "Where's the bar?" line, and we've all felt its undeniable sting.

Here are some useful and benign tactics to help you delicately remove yourself from a conversation while maintaining civility and respect for acquaintances new and old (shhh . . . please don't share these with my guests!):

GRAB THE CLOSEST PERSON YOU KNOW AND REEL HIM INTO THE CONVERSATION

If you can't recall the other person's name or, worse yet, the name of the person to whom you're already talking, lead with a casual "You two know each other, right?" Then quickly reference the topic of conversation before either victim can protest: "We were just talking about . . ." And though you could get busted for not knowing either person's name, the odds of anyone calling you out are slim. So it's worth the potential embarrassment to give it a try. Sometimes introductions will inevitably result in a laconic, forced exchange, at which point you'll give the person you were originally talking to the impetus to come up with his own exit strategy. The bottom line: don't immediately dart for the bar when the conversation slows—first attempt to manage a graceful escape while making all participants comfortable.

POLITELY MENTION THE NEED TO WELCOME A NEW ARRIVAL OR A PASSING GUEST

It is expected and understood that, as the host, you have certain duties, one of which is to work the room and say hi to arriving guests. Simply abbreviate the current conversation by offering your apologies and excusing yourself to fulfill your hosting responsibilities. If you are merely an attendee at this gathering, choose an opportune time to excuse yourself by stating the need to say hello to a guest who just entered the room or is passing by. If you don't know anyone else at the party, you can always utilize a similar approach by offering that you notice the host or hostess "just over there" and must excuse yourself to thank her for her graciousness.

TAKE CARE OF BUSINESS

If you are the host, pardon yourself from the conversation by noting that you must head to the kitchen (or speak to the facility manager) to ensure that the engagement is coming off without a hitch, or conscientiously fill a guest's empty glass at the other side of the room. If you are a guest, wait for the right opportunity to confide that there is an associate in the room whom you must say hello to before he thinks you are avoiding him. By pretending to divulge this little bit of personal information, the person you are trying to escape will actually feel like you are treating him as a confidant.

FIND THE SHRINKING VIOLET

This practice is particularly easy when you are the host, but it can work for guests, too. Mention that you've noticed a lonely soul stranded in the corner for an unacceptable amount of time, and that you've got to bring her into the circle. It is never rude to make another guest feel at home and at ease.

If all else fails, head to the bathroom. Unless you are a woman talking to another woman—for god's sakes, she may end up coming with you!

–71–

UNDERSTAND WINE

GARY VAYNERCHUK

Gary Vaynerchuk is the director of operations at The Wine Library. He is the author of Gary Vaynerchuk's 101 Wines: Guaranteed to Inspire, Delight, and Bring Thunder to Your World *and host of Wine Library TV, on which his Webcast, "The Thunder Show," attracts more than sixty thousand viewers each day.*

Think of the wine world as a mansion. Like most wine drinkers, you are probably living only in your bedroom, with hundreds of other rooms to explore. Yet despite what wine traditionalists may have led you to believe, exploring the world of wine doesn't have to be laborious. In fact, in just one year anyone can become a wine expert.

Expanding your horizons is half the fun—the other half, of course, is the drinking part—but you'll have to start by actually choosing some wines. While the enormous amount of variety can be intimidating, it is also what makes wine so exciting. This leads me to my two guiding principles of wine selection:

RULE #1: DRINK AS MANY DIFFERENT WINES AS YOU CAN

Put aside all the wine geek clutter rattling around in your head and just pick something you've never had before. That's it. Seriously. Selecting a wine should become a thirty-second process, with your guiding principle merely that you should never choose the same wine twice. You wouldn't want to go to the same vacation spot or have the same meal over and over, would you? So skip the Chardonnay or Pinot Noir and go for a Malbec or Petit Verdot. Check out some reds from Portugal, sample the Loire Valley for its Cabernet Franc, and pick up an offering from South America. Don't be scared of wines from Virginia, Texas, or New York either. Even India and China are poised to produce interesting wines; Israel and Lebanon, too. Expand your boundaries, and don't always listen to those who profess to know more than you do—i.e., the "Wine Bullies." This leads me to:

RULE #2: TRUST YOUR OWN PALATE

People traditionally think white wine goes with fish and red wine with meat. This is the most obnoxious rule in the wine industry and a complete fabrication. Nobody can tell me that Greco Di Tufo isn't perfect with pizza, because it is for me. Everyone has a different palate, and what is right for someone else might not be right for you.

If you are still developing your palate and don't yet know what you like, it's time to start figuring things out. Given how many reasonably priced bottles of wine are readily available, you could try tasting a new wine every three to four days without breaking the bank. Or consider starting a monthly tasting group with some friends. If you each bring a bottle to the get-together, you'll be able to try a handful of new wines at a time. But first, some quick advice about purchasing wine:

DO NOT:

1. Fall for the label: There is no correlation between the beauty of the label and the quality of the wine.

2. Blindly follow reviews: Just because it wins awards doesn't mean you'll like it.

3. Assume price equals quality: When you buy an expensive handbag or car, it is probably of higher quality than less expensive options. The same is not true for wine.

Start a journal and take a few notes about each wine you try. The key is to describe the wines in your own language—not the traditional lingo of wine industry experts. For example, rather than "dry" or "fruity," I might describe a wine as tasting like "Big League Chew" or "Riding the Skittles rainbow." These are the flavors that I can relate to; your personal frame of reference will surely be different, but make sure to use it.

Don't get discouraged. For the first few months everything will taste like, well, wine. In my second year tasting wine I tried an Amarone. It tasted just like a Snickers bar. I was so excited because until then I considered myself book smart about wine, but I hadn't actually been able to distinguish flavors. Over time, you, too, will be able to differentiate between flavors, and in one year you will have such a feel for your own palate that you will never again need my advice (or anyone else's).

–72–

STOCK YOUR HOME BAR

RANDE GERBER

> Rande Gerber has opened more than thirty properties
> (nightspots and hotels) around the United States, Europe,
> and Mexico, including The Whiskey, Whiskey Blue, Stone
> Rose, and Underbar, and has launched the Rande Gerber
> Midnight Bar Collection, a line of signature cocktail
> products available at retailers, restaurants, and bars.
> Gerber is married to supermodel Cindy Crawford.

A properly stocked bar can be much more than a place to concoct your favorite libation. It's a place to gather with business associates, neighbors, friends, and family. When entertaining guests, the bar is the perfect place to showcase your personality and taste.

Today's home bar should feature a wide variety of choices. In order to stock your bar quickly and efficiently, you should sit down and make a list of what's important to you. A solid foundation for any good bar is vodka, gin, rum, tequila, scotch, bourbon, cognac, wine, champagne, and beer. In addition, fresh limes, lemons, lemon twists, oranges, and olives will enhance any drink you prepare. Cranberry, fresh orange, and grapefruit juices are also important mixers.

Once you've selected the ingredients, be sure to have the proper tools in your spirit laboratory. You will need a martini shaker and strainer, tall and short straws, and small cocktail napkins. You should also stock toothpicks so your guests aren't fishing the olives out of their glass with their fingers.

Stocking the proper glassware is also important. Red and white wine glasses, martini glasses, tall glasses, rocks glasses, and proper beer glasses are all designed to enhance the beverage experience.

Following are some general guidelines to help you determine what products you may want to stock at your bar. Remember to store additional quantities of these items to avoid running out of your boss's favorite.

- VODKA. Vodka is currently the most popular spirit. There are some very good flavored and infused vodka choices on the market. I recommend stocking at least two different brands.

- GIN. Two brands should be enough.

- RUM. One light and one dark. You may want to add a coconut-flavored rum as well.

- TEQUILA. One silver and one gold are sufficient; however, due to its growing popularity, I like to feature many different brands.

- SCOTCH. Scotch drinkers can be very picky about their brands, so have two types on hand, one blended and one single malt.

- BOURBON. I recommend two types, regular Kentucky bourbon and a high-end single barrel.

- COGNAC. One VSOP and one XO for special occasions.

- WINE. One white and one red. There are so many good afford-able wines to choose from. Take the time to experience a few before deciding on which ones to feature at your bar.

- CHAMPAGNE. This item can be complicated, as real champagne is produced only in the Champagne region of France. All others are technically sparkling wines. Stock a good California sparkling wine and a medium-priced champagne for special celebrations.

- BEER. Bottled beer is best. One domestic and one imported brand will do the trick.

Now you have a foundation for your home bar, though you may want to expand the number of brands you have based on the size and layout of your bar area. And don't be afraid to experiment by adding to your collection. It's a great feeling when you have guests over and you help broaden their beverage knowledge with something you love. Also take into consideration the tastes of your close friends. If you've heard someone talking about a particular spirit or wine they've enjoyed recently, think of how surprised they will be the next time they come over for dinner and you offer them their favorite passion-fruit-infused vodka.

On a final note, don't forget one of the most important pieces to this puzzle: ice. Always stock twice as much ice as you think you'll need. Nothing says, "The party's over. Go home," like running out of ice.

-73-

ACHIEVE FEMALE ORGASM

LAURA BERMAN

*Dr. Laura Berman is the director of the Berman Center,
a sexual-health facility located in Chicago. She is an
assistant clinical professor of psychiatry and obstetrics/
gynecology at the Feinberg School of Medicine at
Northwestern University and the star of Showtime's
documentary* Sexual Healing. *She is a columnist for
the* Chicago Sun-Times *and the author of three books,
including* The Passion Prescription.

Understand your own sexual response first, and you'll get there faster with a partner. Here are some tips:

• DON'T SKIMP ON FANTASY: When it comes to autoeroticism, a little bit of fantasy goes a long way. Conjure up a sexy daydream or picture your favorite celebrity in the buff. As you begin to become aroused, start stimulating the number-one female hot spot—the clitoris.

- THE FEMALE HOT SPOT: The clitoris is much longer than most people think, 10 to 12 centimeters in length, although most of it is internal. The external part of it is located within and near the top of the labia. Stimulation of the clitoris often brings women to powerful orgasms. Try various kinds of stimulation and pressure on this area in order to decipher which feels best. Once you discover what turns you on, you can share it with your partner!

- GOOD VIBRATIONS: A vibrator can truly be a girl's best friend, especially when it comes to speeding up your orgasm. Myths and misconceptions about vibrators abound. Some people believe that vibrator use will "deaden" the senses, or make men obsolete. Not so! Using a vibrator can actually increase a woman's sexual desire and sexual response. Moreover, a vibrator is not a replacement for the intimacy and attraction that exists between lovers. Indeed, it can function as a great tool for re-establishing passion and excitement in a relationship.

FOR FASTER ORGASM WITH INTERCOURSE:

- THE MASCULINE MISTAKE: Many men do not realize that only 30 percent of women reach orgasm through intercourse alone. In fact, only the outermost third of a woman's vagina is sensitive—so the usual ins-and-outs of sex may leave her feeling unsatisfied. Luckily, there are a few tried-and-true ways to help the woman along:

  - *Don't rush through foreplay.* There is something to be said for passionate quickies, but for the most part, women want and need foreplay. Sensual kissing, erotic massages, and oral and manual stimulation are all important parts of great sex. With the right amount of foreplay, the woman will be more lubricated, further along in her arousal process, and more likely to achieve orgasm through intercourse.

- *The best positions.* Some positions lend themselves more easily to female pleasure. The CAT (Coital Alignment Technique) is a variation on the missionary position where the man lifts up and over the woman upon entry so that the base of his penis and pelvic bone are against her clitoris. Then, with consistent rocking motion, she receives maximum clitoral stimulation. The "woman-on-top" position gives her the ability to control the thrusting, and it again stimulates that all-important spot. Other positions, such as doggy-style, allow for the woman or her partner to stimulate her clitoris from behind during intercourse. You can also use a small vibrator that can fit between the two of you. An even better option might be one of the popular vibrating things that fit around the base of the penis, providing hands-free stimulation during intercourse.

- THE RIGHT TOUCH: There are endless possibilities for stimulating the clitoris, both manually and orally. Some women enjoy direct contact, while for others indirect touching is better. For women who prefer less direct contact, a partner can try moving his fingers in a figure eight, since it simultaneously engages many nerve endings. The figure eight can be small, moving mostly around the clitoris, or large, to work the entire length of the vulva. For women who like direct pressure on the clitoris, one or two fingers can be used to tap or rub it constantly. Many women also enjoy having their vaginal opening massaged, as it is full of sensation-friendly nerve endings. Some women find the perineum (the area between the anus and the vulva) arousing as well.

- ORAL PERFORMANCE: Soft and wet, the tongue is often the best tool for achieving female orgasm. While the man works her clitoris with his mouth, he can insert one or two fingers into her vagina with a gentle thrusting motion. By tilting them upward slightly, he can try to hit her G-spot. The G-spot can be found one or two inches in on her vagina. It feels like a spongy bump. Discovering how to manipulate the G-spot (it works best if she explores on her own first) will also help facilitate orgasms and make them come quicker!

Women, if you don't like something, speak up! If you want to try a new position or play out a fantasy, don't be afraid to share these thoughts. Great sex begins with forthright communication—after that, a little technique can go a long way.

-74-

BAKE A CAKE

WARREN BROWN

Warren Brown is a lawyer turned baker. He owns and operates five CakeLove bakery cafés in the Washington, D.C., area. Brown hosted Sugar Rush *on Food Network and is the author of* CakeLove: How to Bake Cakes from Scratch.

aking a cake is not as difficult as you may think. If you follow just a few critical steps you'll be on your way to impressing yourself and the lucky ones you greet with your next home-made treat.

Any time you're in the kitchen you must have a plan. Baking is no exception; in fact, it's considered the most precise of all culinary arts. But don't let the science behind baking intimidate you. If you carefully measure the ingredients you'll be halfway home. Mixing the batter is the remaining battle, and all that takes is good ol' patience and practice.

Keep in mind that cake batter is a combination of ingredients suspended around air. Air is critical—without it your cake will have no height and its texture will be too dense. Some recipes capture air between ingredients while the batter is being mixed. Other recipes rely on carbon dioxide released from baking powder or baking soda to aerate the cake. But however you get it there, the air won't be able to do its job if the ingredients aren't measured properly.

The easiest way to advance your cake-baking skills is to use a scale when measuring the flour. Avoid the common "scoop and level" method—flour typically gets compacted when cup measures are dipped into the bag. I always sift my flour immediately before measuring it, too. The sifter breaks up the flour and reduces clumping in the mixer bowl. The type of flour you use is a personal preference determined by the taste, texture, and flavor each will yield. I favor unbleached all-purpose flour over cake flour.

One of the common barriers to successful baking is a lack of proper equipment, particularly a mixer, which many home cooks don't have. So below is a recipe that doesn't require a mixer. It comes together in less than five minutes, bakes in about twenty-five, and, most important, the result is buttery and delicious! Baking from scratch has *never* been easier or faster.

VANILLA CAKE WITH CHOCOLATE GLAZE

REQUIRED EQUIPMENT
Large bowl

1-quart plastic container with lid

Whisk

Sifter or wire-mesh strainer

2 cake pans or cupcake pans

Paper cups for 24 cupcakes

Nonreactive (stainless steel or glass) small mixing bowl

Heavy-bottomed sauce pan

VANILLA CAKE
7 ounces (1¼ cups) unbleached all-purpose flour

12 ounces (1½ cups) extra-fine granulated sugar

2 ounces (¾ cup) confectioner's sugar

1 tablespoon baking powder

½ teaspoon salt

6 ounces (1½ sticks) unsalted butter, melted

1 cup milk

1 tablespoon heavy cream

2 teaspoons vanilla extract

4 large eggs

1 egg yolk

1. Preheat the oven to 350°F (conventional)/335°F (convection).
2. Sift the flour into the bowl and whisk in the other dry ingredients to combine.
3. Microwave the butter for 35 to 40 seconds, until melted.
4. Measure the wet ingredients into the plastic container. Seal the container and shake well to combine thoroughly.
5. Whisk the liquid ingredients into the dry ingredients. Combine thoroughly.
6. Pour the batter into 2 cake pans lined with parchment paper—don't grease the sides of the pans. For cupcakes, fill paper-cup-lined cupcake pans about three quarters of the way.
7. Bake for 25 minutes.

8. Remove from the oven when the tops are golden brown and a wooden skewer poked in the center comes out clean. Cool thoroughly on a heat-resistant surface.
9. Run a thin metal spatula around the rim to release the cake and invert it onto a plate.
10. Serve with a dusting of powdered sugar, or chocolate glaze (below).

CHOCOLATE GLAZE

1 cup 60 percent bittersweet chocolate

1 cup heavy cream

2 teaspoons vanilla extract

1. Carefully chop or cut the chocolate into small pieces and place in the small mixing bowl.
2. Combine the heavy cream and vanilla extract in a 1- or 2-quart heavy-bottomed sauce pan and bring to a simmer over medium heat.
3. Pour the cream over the chocolate and let sit for 10 to 20 seconds. (This allows the heat to loosen up the chocolate.) Gently whisk to combine the cream and the chocolate.
4. Let the chocolate cool until it doesn't look too loose (about 5 minutes), then dip the top of each cupcake (down to the cupcake-paper edge) into the chocolate.
5. For optimal taste, serve the cake at room temperature.

You did it!

–75–

GARDEN

JON CARLOFTIS

Jon Carloftis is a garden designer and the author of Beyond
the Windowsill *and* First a Garden. *He is a member of
HGTV's TrendSmart Panel and has designed rooftop
gardens for many celebrities, including Julianne Moore,
Mike Myers, and Edward Norton.*

They say that some things can't be rushed; gardening is usually
on that list. Try telling that to a New Yorker with a penthouse
ready to entertain guests under the stars. I learned to create
any kind of garden more quickly by using these simple steps:

1. HAVE A PLAN. Don't just go buying things in bloom because
when the blooms are over, so is the garden. Visualize the big picture; if you can't do this, have a professional help you with a plan.
With an end in sight, things seem to fall into place. Begin with the
outer plantings to create a "room." Four simple trees at each corner can define the space. Will you be using the garden for dining,
relaxing, cooking, or perhaps just viewing from inside? Keep your
plan in mind throughout every decision.

2. GET ORGANIZED. Whether you have a balcony or terrace in the city or a multiple-acre plot in the country, work goes quicker when you don't have to hunt for tools and materials every time the urge to garden hits you. A closet, small outbuilding, well-thought-out wall in the garage, or even a waterproof storage box that doubles as a seat will work just fine for storage.

3. SIMPLIFY AS MUCH AS POSSIBLE IN EVERY CATEGORY. As far as gadgets go, do you really need them or do they take up valuable space? When designing the garden, one plant of every variety works in an arboretum but usually not in a private space. Find the plants that work well in your climate/zone and make them the "bones" of your garden. Continuity is pleasing to the eye and indigenous plants always make sense when it comes to long-term care later on.

4. START FROM THE GROUND UP. Find out what your soil needs and make the correct adjustments. Everything comes from the earth, and this is the most important part of the equation.

5. WATER, WATER, WATER, ESPECIALLY IN THE BEGINNING OF THE PLANTING SEASON. Deep watering establishes deep roots and will save time as well as precious water later on when the months are hot and dry. If water supplies are an issue in your area (and they are becoming an issue everywhere), choose planters that don't require exorbitant amounts of water.

6. FERTILIZE ON A REGULAR BASIS. Each time it rains or whenever you water, nutrients are leached out of the soil, especially in containers. It took me years to learn the importance of fertilizing, and as a result my gardens have never looked better. Organic fertilizers are kinder to mother earth and it makes sense not to use chemicals. In terms of frequency, for annuals, every two weeks

with a water-soluble fertilizer; for perennials, shrubs, and trees, do it in the spring with an all-purpose slow-release fertilizer; and for interior plants, fertilize during the growing season and not in the winter months.

7. LEARN THE TRICKS OF THE TRADE. Sometimes an over-the-top urn at the end of a simple green hedge can have as much oomph and drama as a labor-intensive, time-consuming perennial border. Less is always more when it comes to garden design. Also, to fill in empty spaces for a quicker, lush look, plant inexpensive seeds. Cleome, cosmos, forget-me-nots, and bachelor's buttons do a fantastic job of adding color and texture quickly in the garden. Many types of flowers will self-seed each year, which will save you time and money when gardening next year.

-76-

SOLVE A CROSSWORD

TYLER HINMAN

Tyler Hinman has won the American Crossword Puzzle Tournament for four consecutive years (2005–2008). He was a star of the 2006 documentary film Wordplay.

Ah, the crossword puzzle. It's challenging and it's fun. It can also be a good way to impress strangers on trains, but only if you're skillful and quick.

You can't be a fast solver before you can complete puzzles, so the first step is to solve lots of puzzles. You're not going to get better by reading the dictionary. Instead, take a crack at your newspaper's puzzle every day, even if you feel it's too hard. Look up answers on the Internet or in the next day's paper, but not before you've made an honest effort to solve it on your own. If you regularly solve a puzzle that increases in difficulty as the week progresses, you'll have a good benchmark for how you're coming along. I tried to solve for a month before I completed the Tuesday (second easiest) *New York Times* puzzle, and a full year before I conquered Friday. Solving puzzles was all I had to do to gain this skill!

More quick tips:

- As you solve more, you'll naturally get in tune with how crossword makers and editors think, thus allowing you to see through the wordplay and other tricks prevalent in harder puzzles.

- You'll also pick up lots of crosswordese, words that may or may not appear in conversation but which enjoy immense popularity in puzzles due to their puzzlemaker-friendly letter combinations: ANOA (a small buffalo), ESNE (an Anglo-Saxon laborer) . . . you get the idea. Constructors try to avoid these overused words, but solid knowledge of this vocabulary will still give you a few gimmes.

- Keep an eye out for a puzzle's theme, something that ties together some answers of the puzzle, usually the longest. Not all crosswords have themes, but most do, and figuring out the theme can help you take down those long answers. Occasionally, this theme will be a screwy gimmick, like putting a symbol or multiple letters in a single square, so be on the lookout

- If you're really stuck, rethink an answer you've already written. I've wasted many minutes on puzzles because I was married to a wrong answer. Or try putting the puzzle down, doing a nonintellectual activity for a while, and coming back to it. It's amazing what a fresh start can do.

So now you can solve any crossword that comes your way. How do you get faster? Practice, of course, is still important, but here are some other things to try:

- Use pencil. Erasing is faster than scribbling over errors.
- Don't go through the clues in order, i.e., all the acrosses and

then all the downs. If you solve an answer, read the clues to the crossing answers. No matter how easy or hard the clue, you have a much better chance of getting the right answer quickly if you have at least one letter to help you. Only move on to a blank space if you get stuck.

- Start with fill-in-the-blank clues, as these usually are among the easier clues in a puzzle, with the least potential for trickery and misinterpretation. Plus, they're easy to spot with a quick scan through the clue list.

- Start with short answers. Longer answers are more likely to be part of a tricky theme, a multiple-word phrase, and/or clued with wordplay or difficult trivia. Sometimes you'll be lucky enough to solve a big answer right away, but usually you'll want some help from the smaller crossing entries.

- If you're really serious, get a stopwatch and time yourself. Strive to beat your best time for each level of difficulty.

- If you're really, really serious, read the next clue at the same time that you're writing an answer. This is hard, but if you've become very skilled you may need only a glance at that next clue to solve it and keep your writing uninterrupted. (Needless to say, the integrity of your handwriting markedly deteriorates at this point. Don't worry about it.)

-77-
FIND THE PERFECT PRESENT

LASH FARY

Lash Fary is the CEO of Distinctive Assets, a Los Angeles–based entertainment marketing company that provides gift baskets for events including the Grammys and the Tony Awards. He is the author of Fabulous Gifts: Hollywood's Gift Guru Reveals the Secret to Giving the Perfect Present.

Whether you're shopping for a celebrity, your favorite aunt, your dad, or your accountant, the rules for finding the perfect present as quickly and efficiently as possible are simple and finite. And they all start with being proactive. Gifts are an individual expression of both you and the recipient, so they deserve your time and attention. Here are a few basic streamlining tactics to minimize the input and maximize your results.

KNOW YOUR AUDIENCE

Many people are overwhelmed by the prospect of shopping for gifts simply because they aren't clear about what they need and for whom until it's too late to make the best decisions. There's a reason why every efficiency expert out there recommends lists. After all, it's worked for Santa all these years. Sit down (right now!) and make a list of your gift needs over the next six to twelve months. Next to each giftee's name and the occasion, quickly brainstorm about that person. What are his or her likes, hobbies, favorite colors, favorite athletes/celebrities, preferred destinations, secret obsessions, passions, and so on? What is his or her personality type? In other words, is your giftee conservative or daring, mature and stuffy, or young and frivolous? Now that you've put pen to paper, are there any immediate gift ideas that spring to mind? If not, don't fret. The point of advance planning is that you are no longer dependent on last-minute "it's good enough" type shopping. Before you flip through your next magazine/catalog or as you're walking through those magical doors at the mall, review your list. You'll be surprised at the amazing ideas that will leap out and inspire you.

JUST DO IT

Whenever you find something that you think would be ideal for someone on your list, don't procrastinate. Buy it, wrap it, and tag it! Unless you're purchasing a perishable item, don't put off the inevitable. You'll save time obsessing over it in the coming weeks, not to mention sparing yourself another trip back to the mall. Similarly, whenever you are out buying something for yourself (or shopping online), review your list and find at least one present you can also order to satisfy an upcoming gift need for someone else. In addition to saving time, you'll save a little money on the shipping. Plus, many stores and websites offer complimentary wrapping, so take advantage of outsourcing this task. You can always add your own personal touches to spruce up the presentation.

BE PREPARED

Establish a "gift area" in your home. It can be as simple as a shelf in the coat closet, a corner of the attic, or a spare drawer in a cabinet. Stock it with wrapping paper, ribbon, bows, tags, bags, note cards, tape, and tissue paper, as well as those proactive purchases you've been making! By building up your supply inventory once, you'll save time scrambling around to deal with all these presentation details at the last minute on dozens of isolated occasions. Another big time-saver is to stock up on "standard" gifts such as candles, boxes of gift cards, and wine. Having these "basics" labeled and ready to go at a moment's notice will save you time and stress for those last-minute party invitations and occasions that slip through the cracks.

-78-

HOLIDAY SHOP

PACO UNDERHILL

*Paco Underhill is a retail anthropologist and
the founder and CEO of Envirosell, a retail consulting
firm. He is the author of* Why We Buy:
The Science of Shopping.

B y the end of Thanksgiving dinner many families have exhausted all safe topics of conversation. So on Friday, to avoid talking about politics, money, or someone's new tattoos, Americans go shopping on what has become the busiest retail shopping day of the year.

Stores are crowded, mall parking lots are overrun, and the heavy meal from the day before makes us lethargic and crabby. What's more, in the month between Thanksgiving and Christmas, all the rules change. Ignorant men drum up the courage to shop the fragrance counter, and many a mom, sister, wife, or girlfriend steps into a consumer electronics store for the first time of the year. With shopping lists that extend to the floor and so many elements conspiring against you, the holiday shopper, success often rests on how well prepared you are before you walk into the store.

That's why it's important to take a step back and think about your ultimate purpose before devising a game plan. Holiday gifts are about exchanging tokens of your esteem for other people. It is not about how much you spend, but the thought you put into it. So before shopping, determine what it is that you want the gift to say . . . I love you, I like you, I am proud of you.

I have a disabled friend who lives on Social Security. Even on her limited budget she gives great, beautifully wrapped presents. Almost every Christmas, she gives me something unique with ginger in it—tea, cookies, soap. I have all the neckties and shirts I need, but I love ginger—the tea gets drunk, the cookies eaten, and the soap used. Can you say the same about your gifts?

Here are a few pointers to get you in and out of the stores quickly this holiday season, while also making sure you head home with all the right gifts:

1. Make a list of people to buy for. Jot ideas or specific gifts on your list for easy reference. Don't buy for anyone who isn't on your list—there must be a reason why he or she didn't make it the first time.

2. Time it right. Never shop when you are hungry or tired. Our judgment functions best at 10:30 AM. At 5:30 PM we can be indecisive and make compromises we will regret.

3. Be careful about the thrill of buying—it can be a sign of shopping sickness. What is important is the satisfaction gained in using or giving what you have bought.

4. If you want to give something unique and original, visit your local independent merchant. Chain stores can only buy from suppliers that can fill their shelves.

5. Resist the urge to take advantage of the abundant sales; don't buy things for yourself.

6. Remember that gifts don't have to be things—they can be experiences: theater tickets, massages, nail treatments, or airplane tickets.

7. This is a stressful time for everyone, including store employees. When shopping, be friendly, look people in the eye, and, if appropriate, thank those who help you. Good manners and eye contact get remembered and can make your experience run more smoothly.

8. If something doesn't go right, ask politely for a correction, but if you don't get what you want, take your business elsewhere. In most cases the aggravation of the confrontation isn't worth it and you'll get more satisfaction dissuading others by contributing to negative buzz.

-79-

SEND CHRISTMAS CARDS

ANN HODGMAN

Ann Hodgman is the author of numerous books,

including I Saw Mommy Kicking Santa Claus:

The Ultimate Holiday Survival Guide.

I n my ceaseless desire to streamline the Christmas process, I originally thought it might be best to get rid of Christmas cards altogether. Yet in the years when I was able to get it together to send cards, I was always so heartened by the response that I chose to keep the custom going. I decided, however, that I had to figure out a less insane way of doing them. Away went the personal notes with each one! Away went the trip to the post office to get special holiday stamps! And in came the following modifications, which turned Christmas cards into a fun ritual instead of a horrible chore.

HIRE OUT THE ENVELOPE ADDRESSING

No one thinks this part of the job is fun. And who cares what the envelope looks like? It just gets thrown away. If your kids are old enough to write, they'll probably be delighted to get paid to address your envelopes for you. (It's a job that can be done in front of the TV, as long as they're careful to double-check each finished address.) If you don't have kids of the right age, why not hire a neighborhood teenager to do this chore? It's much easier than babysitting, and it gives artistic girls a chance to practice different handwriting and put little circles over the *i*'s.

Also, consider hiring someone—again, a kid is a source of good cheap labor—to create a mailing list on your computer, so that in future years all you have to do is print up labels.

DO IT ONLINE

If you're sending out pictures of your kids, there's absolutely no reason not to use an online photo service to take care of your Christmas card photos. Send them a digital photo, tell them how many copies you want, and pick out a card to have the photo inserted into. They'll send the finished photo cards to you, and then all you have to do is mail them.

CUT DOWN ON YOUR LIST

If you're sending out more than one hundred cards a year, you're in way over your head. No one has that many important friends and business associates. And if, somehow, you do, then you don't need to stay in touch with all of them every year. Rotate your list.

Start by trimming people who live nearby. Why do they need a card when they see you all the time? Get rid of all the business-related cards that aren't absolutely essential in keeping you afloat financially. Think of all the guilt you'll be able to save the recipients—now they won't owe you a card! Be a little ruthless about acquaintances you don't love. If you're sending a card only out of habit, let those people go. Save Christmas cards for the people you love and the people to whom cards will bring joy. The rest is pointless.

SEND YOUR CHRISTMAS CARDS AFTER CHRISTMAS

This is what I do. I'm putting it last because so many people feel that a Christmas card should arrive by—well—Christmas. But why? The point is to connect with your friends and family once a year. Why not do it after Christmas, when everyone is feeling low? I notice that more and more friends are sending New Year's cards, which I hope takes hold as a custom. It's more secular, it prolongs the holiday feeling, and, not least, it will make your life in December a lot easier.

TRAVEL

-80-

PLAN A VACATION

BARBARA MESSING

Barbara Messing is a travel expert and vice president at Hotwire.com, a leading discount travel site owned by Expedia Inc.

Today's technology makes it easier than ever to book your next vacation with a few simple mouse clicks. But with millions of different rates and choices out there, navigating your way to the vacation of a lifetime can be confusing and time-consuming. The fact is, the cost of travel varies wildly based on timing and demand, and trying to figure out the best time to book can feel like a guessing game. But don't be deterred—armed with the following tips and tricks, you'll be ready to get where you want to go faster with some extra money in your pocket.

WHERE DO YOU WANT TO GO TODAY?

Start by creating a wish list of places you'd like to visit. Be sure to include everything from your dream vacations to local trips and weekend getaways. Whether African safaris, French wine tours,

Galapagos yachting, Los Angeles spas, or Berkshires leaf peeping, everyone has a trip that captures their travel imagination. Now you'll know before you start what deals and destinations to look out for. With so many great places to go in the world, why not let a great price lead your vacation planning?

TIMING IS EVERYTHING, SO TAKE ADVANTAGE OF ONLINE TRAVEL-PLANNING TOOLS

Rates can vary dramatically with even a one-day change in your itinerary. But pricing out multiple itineraries can be time-consuming. Luckily, most travel websites offer handy search tools to help you find low rates in no time. For example, try a "flexible date search," which lets you find any available lower fares. If a Friday fare is too high, you may be able to pay half the price by traveling the day before. Some sites even let you search a thirty-day range. Since one of the most time-consuming elements in planning a trip is finding your desired itinerary at the right price, this tool will help get you on your way faster.

SIGN UP FOR E-MAIL TRAVEL NEWSLETTERS

Subscribe to e-newsletters from major travel websites to get last-minute deals sent right to your inbox. You will be shocked at some of the absurdly low prices you'll see. Look for deals to your top destinations, but be open-minded. If the price is right, a beach vacation will be a blast whether it's in Hawaii or the Caribbean. Travel newsletters also let you know about new hotels in destinations with introductory rates, the latest hot spots, and package trips that do all the legwork for you. I subscribe to everything I can because I love to know what is out there.

BE THE CONTRARIAN

High demand causes prices to spike, so unless budget is not an issue for you, don't follow the crowds. When everyone else is hitting the beach, head for the mountains. Vegas midweek and in the summer is just as fun as on the busier days, but at a fraction of the cost. Also take advantage of the "shoulder season." This is the time of year—which varies by destination—in between the low season (empty rooms, but possibly suboptimal vacation conditions) and high season (the masses are there and prices are high). Europe is lovely in October, with mild weather, fewer crowds, and significantly lower prices. And if you can avoid school vacation weeks (Christmas, Easter), you will have your pick of destinations.

A LITTLE FLEXIBILITY CAN REALLY PAY OFF

Travel the weekend before or after a major holiday. Check alternate airports to see how that impacts fares—the drive may be a bit longer, but the dollars saved will make it worth your time. If possible, search for flights on Tuesdays and Wednesdays, when many airlines release special fares and promotions.

Finally, when you see a great deal, book it. There is nothing worse than missing out on a trip to a place you've longed to visit. Once you've booked your getaway, stop spending time worrying about all the pretrip planning and start thinking about your next adventure, eliminating even the chance of post-vacation blues upon your return.

-81-

PICK UP A FOREIGN LANGUAGE

BOB ARNOT

Dr. Bob Arnot is a physician and foreign correspondent known for reporting from hot spots around the world. He was a correspondent for CBS and NBC and he is now the star of Dr. Danger. *Arnot speaks eight languages: English, Arabic, Swahili, German, French, Spanish, Shona, and Japanese.*

As a physician and journalist, knowing the local language has not only been the key to getting the story, it has saved my life. I was imprisoned in the Congo by rebels while reporting on conflict diamonds but talked my way out of danger in Swahili. Knowing the local language also dramatically changes my storytelling. Instead of standing in front of a crowd of "foreign"-looking people, I dive in and talk to them in their language as if they were my neighbors.

I've developed a go-to method for quickly picking up any language, and I swear it works no matter how incapable you think you may be. Here's what to do:

1. BUY A GRAMMAR BOOK. By learning to conjugate verbs, you multiply your learning power by a factor of at least ten. Simply learn the base word and from there you can put together dozens of sentences. Learn one verb, conjugate it properly, and you already sound like a pro. Learn the personal pronouns, conjunctions, and prepositions so you can immediately start to construct erudite sentences.

2. BUY A GREAT SMALL DICTIONARY OR VOCABULARY BOOK. Underline the words you are trying to learn. This way, if you go back to the language years later, you can return to that same book. Memorize one hundred verbs and one thousand nouns as quickly as possible and ask friends to quiz you.

3. BUY A DVD. This is the most indispensable part. If you're dead set against memorization, this is what you want. Push yourself through the entire program, picking up as much as you possibly can. I've found this to be the best leap to fluency. You can often hear the sentences in your head from the program. It's highly rewarding and allows you to quickly see how your new vocabulary works. Keep the DVD in your luggage. I watch the DVD on the flight so I'm ready to roll when I get there. This July it was Afghanistan and the language was Pashto.

4. GO TO A GREAT LANGUAGE SCHOOL. Look for one that teaches the equivalent of the "Queen's English," where the diction is crystal clear and the words crisp and easy to understand.

Armed with a modest vocabulary you can now express yourself to the local population of a country—or, if at home, to an unsuspecting person who speaks the language you are trying to learn. Most people wait years to develop perfect grammar and comprehension before starting to speak—and then never do. The most efficient learning is through error correction. So go ahead—throw out your best sentences with reckless abandon. With luck, the recipient will be charmed. The corrections you get will stick to your memory like glue. You'll remember for a lifetime how the maître d' taught you a perfect new sentence.

And two more tips for faster language learning:

1. SPEAK IT. Locals often want to practice their English and won't give you a chance to reinforce your own new language skills, so try this: Ask for something in superfast English. When they give you an astonished look and say they don't understand, slip into their language. You'll get a look of relief!

2. LEARN CONVERSATIONS. First, learn all the greetings. Then learn to ask about their family and children. Then learn about a favorite hobby. Lead the discussion into subjects where you can shine. Learn the vocabulary for a series of conversations. One day, as if by magic, you'll find that not only do you understand the response to your questions but you have become fluent—one of the greatest thrills there is.

–82–

PACK

LISA LINDBLAD

Lisa Lindblad is the founder of Lisa Lindblad Travel Design, a New York–based company that creates customized travel experiences. Travel & Leisure magazine has listed her as one of America's top five Super Agents from 2003 to 2007.

Packing well and quickly is an exercise in mental rigor, emotional discipline, and physical dexterity. The mental part requires anticipating climatic and activity parameters; emotional discipline demands the courage to stick to your packing choices; and physical dexterity will mean packing right to ensure that your clothes will see you through your trip looking great.

BEFORE YOU BEGIN:

- Call the airline to find out baggage weight and size restrictions
- Go online to check the weather forecast at your destination
- Set up an area to lay out your clothes and coordinate outfits

- Stick with two basic colors for your travel wardrobe and add items of color for accent
- Choose fabrics that resist wrinkling, such as rayon and denim

THE STAPLES:

- Pack at the last minute; you will take less
- Permanently keep a list in your wheeled suitcase of those things you can't live without on a trip, as well as your passport
- Keep a dop kit (toiletry kit) stocked with bare essentials—toothbrush and toothpaste, lotions, Chap Stick—those things you always need with you. For example, I always have bandages and Neosporin, but for you it might be eyeliner and mascara!
- Keep a few large plastic bags in your suitcase (for dirty clothes or to hold sweaters or toiletries)

CLOTHES TO BRING (ADJUST FOR WEATHER AND LENGTH OF TRIP):

- Two pairs of shoes—one walking and one flat for evening that can double as "nice" day shoes as well
- Jeans
- Black pants
- Khakis
- Skirt
- Sweats for travel, or as pajamas or exercise clothes
- Tops, both sleeveless and long-sleeved, that can be layered and, if necessary, double for day or night wear
- Sweater or light jacket

- Scarf or shawl for warmth and color
- Sarong—you'd be amazed by how versatile it can be. Use it as a tablecloth, skirt, shawl, turban, or cover-up.
- Rain jacket
- Everyday undies plus a pair of silk long underwear if there is a chance of cold weather
- Socks

EXTRAS:

- Ear plugs and/or eye mask
- Universal converter
- Camera and battery charger
- Book/iPod/deck of cards for flight or solo evenings
- Baby pillow

PACKING TECHNIQUE

Always pack as much as you can in your rolling suitcase and hand-carry as little as possible. Remember that shoes should always go on the bottom of your suitcase in shoe bags. To make the most of your space and avoid wrinkling your clothes, roll them before packing them. Any flat clothes should be interwoven with plastic cleaner's bags between each layer.

The final key to packing quickly and successfully is to realize that your suitcase does not need to be full on departure—it will be full when you return! Just make sure to fill the empty space with bubble wrap so that your clothes don't shift during travel.

—83—

GET THROUGH
AIRPORT SECURITY

JAMES WYSONG

James Wysong was a flight attendant for eighteen years. He writes a weekly column at Tripso.com and MSNBC.com. Wysong is the author of four books, including Flying High with a Frank Steward: More Air Travel Tips and Tales *from the Flight Crew.*

T SA doesn't stand for Thousands Standing Around, although sometimes that seems appropriate. It stands for Transportation Security Administration, and if you have dealt with airport security recently, you know it means a long wait.

Nobody likes waiting, then being told to remove some of his clothes, or watching as other passengers ahead of her take an agonizingly long time to be searched.

The lines at security alone are probably enough to turn you off from air travel. In my case, I know that the shortest distance between two points is not the line that I choose. Just as I get close to the front, some complication arises, while all the other lines are moving briskly. Then, as I switch lines, the new one freezes up and the one I left starts moving. But there are certain tricks of the trade that can get you through a bit more quickly and comfortably.

Here are ten tips to help you get through airport security faster:

1. BE UP TO DATE. One day, gels aren't allowed at all, and the next, you need a plastic bag to hold three-ounce containers for each liquid item. The only constant in airline security is change. Before you fly, go to www.tsa.gov and get the latest rules and prohibited items.

2. CUT OUT THE HASSLE. Put all sharp objects or electrical devices you don't need in flight into your checked luggage, where such items are permitted.

3. TAKE IT OFF. Remove anything from your person that is remotely metallic, such as jewelry, watches, and coins, and put them in your carry-on bag that goes through the X-ray machine. This way, you won't set off the metal detector or risk forgetting items you put in the plastic tray.

4. PICK A BOOK AND STICK WITH IT. Bring a book—better yet, bring this book to pass the time.

5. STRIDE RIGHT. Walk through the metal detector in one brisk stride. Stopping halfway, brushing up against the side, or walking through slowly often causes false alarms. If the alarm goes off on your first time through, you get only one more try before the full search, so double-check everything in your pockets and on your person.

6. TAKE NOTES. If you frequently set off the metal detector, listen and pay attention as the screener wands you. If your buttons trigger the alarm, next time wear different attire.

7. HAVE A PLAN OF ATTACK. The most annoying thing about the long lines are the people who have been in line for an hour who suddenly get confused or lost when it is their time to go through. Watch the people in front of you and be ready for your turn. Pull your laptop out of the bag, take your shoes off, and don't forget to put that cell phone elsewhere, for it will trigger the magnetometer.

8. BE SPECIAL. If you fly often enough, you should contact your airline and sign up to be a premium passenger. This allows you access to shorter lines and could shave an average of 50 percent from the wait time. It involves an initial hassle of a background check and a multiple form application, but could be well worth it.

9. DON'T CAUSE A SCENE. I know it's frustrating to be singled out, but that tantrum you are about to throw could delay your journey another thirty minutes. You will be sent through every level of security check they have, just on principle.

10. TUNE OUT. Put on your MP3 player with your favorite music and enjoy the show taking place before you. People are naturally amusing, and the music adds a special touch to the comedy of life. It's like an ad-lib performance of synchronized swimmers. Everyone will look at you oddly as you laugh, but who cares?

-84-

NAVIGATE A NEW CITY

MARYBETH BOND

Marybeth Bond is the author of numerous books, including National Geographic's Best Girlfriends Getaways Worldwide, 50 Best Girlfriends Getaways in North America, *and* Gutsy Women. *She has found her way through cities in seventy-six countries on six continents on foot, bicycles, rickshaws, and elephant back.*

Proficient travel skills are often developed through trial and error, but most people waste time and money before they learn from their mistakes. Here's how to navigate a new city easily without wasting time:

1. Preparation is critical. Look online or buy a guidebook before you start planning your trip. Peruse the destination city's website; most will highlight "must-see" attractions, shopping districts, restaurants, theaters, museums, art galleries, and the most lovely parks and diverse neighborhoods for strolling. Check out the special events calendar on city websites to learn about any music festivals, free opera in the park, parades, and other cultural events.

Order the free visitor's guidebook. When you do an online city search, use the terms "Convention and Visitor's Bureau" and "Tourist Board." Also, look at what tour companies have to offer; they cover the highlights that most visitors want to see. Determine what's available, prioritize your interests, and plan an itinerary around those places and events. You should now be able to calculate how many days you'll need in the city.

2. Hotel location is paramount for easy navigation and safety, so do some research before you plunk down your credit card for accommodations. Locate your desired hotel on a map to ensure its proximity to restaurants, theaters, museums, and major shopping areas, and give serious consideration to how you'd like to move around the city. Do you want to use public transportation? If so, select a hotel located near a major subway station and/or bus stops. But first check to make sure that the city's public transportation system is extensive enough to easily get you to the places you want to see. If you stay in the center of the action you can usually walk to major attractions and avoid complicated public transportation (which often requires exact change) and expensive cabs.

3. Think about whether you really need to rent a car. Hotel parking in the city center can be exorbitantly expensive. In most cases car rental is necessary only if you wish to spend a few days in the countryside. If overseas, consider whether you will need to drive on a different side of the street than at home and, if so, whether you are comfortable with that. Also, be realistic about your comfort level reading street signs in a foreign language.

4. Before you leave, buy a good map of your destination city at a bookstore that has a reputable travel department. Look for specialized maps geared to one area—such as the Michigan Avenue district in Chicago. You don't need to memorize the whole city,

but you want to familiarize yourself with areas of interest before leaving so that you spend less time fiddling around with the map like a typical tourist when you arrive.

5. Consider how you'll get from the airport to your hotel. Read the transportation section of the city's website, or call your hotel and ask for their recommendation.

6. Once you've arrived in the new city and settled in at your hotel, take a bus tour to get an overview of neighborhoods and tourist attractions. You can return later on your own to visit areas of interest more deeply.

7. Ask for help. Your best source of on-the-spot information will be local residents. They maneuver around the city every day and know the commuter patterns and the pitfalls of each mode of transportation. Before you leave your hotel, tell the front-desk clerk or concierge where you are headed and ask if you can walk it. Inquire about where the bus stop or taxi stand is located and whether you'll need correct change.

The more you prepare before you arrive, the easier it will be to navigate your destination city and avoid the pitfalls of inexperienced travelers.

–85–

MAKE YOUR CAR RUN

JIMMY SHINE

Jimmy Shine is the star of TLC's Hard Shine *reality
television series and lead fabricator at SO-CAL
Speed Shop in Pomona, California.*

Man has always loved to go fast. In ancient times fast runners
and horses were highly treasured and envied for their speed.
Little has changed. Naturally, as modes of transportation
have evolved, we have continued to seek higher and higher performance from our now-mechanized transport, and for most of us,
that means a car.

In the early days, the need for speed often meant completely
tearing down the engine and building it up again. Fortunately, for
the majority of cars on the road today, squeezing out a few more
horses is far easier. Power gains in the range of 5 to 15 percent are
readily available today, whether you drive a hot rod, muscle car, or
any new vehicle on the market.

BASIC COMBUSTION ENGINE FUNCTION

An engine is nothing more than a big pump. It sucks in air and spits out exhaust. Increase its ability to take in air and kick out exhaust, and you end up with a faster car.

Okay, maybe that's a bit too basic. In between the inhaling of air and expelling of exhaust, the engine mixes the fresh air with a vaporized fuel, which is then forced into a cylinder. Once in the cylinder, the air/fuel mixture is compressed and then ignited by the spark plug—the energy from the resulting explosion is the power that moves the vehicle. After that, the spent gases are forced out and the process starts all over again.

INCREASING PERFORMANCE

Modern combustion engines are efficient and smart, utilizing fuel injection and other technologies. Through their computers, modern vehicles monitor an engine's performance constantly. A modern vehicle's computer measures the amount of air coming into the intake system, monitors the spent gases in the exhaust, and adds the perfect amount of fuel for efficient operation. So if you increase the amount of air that goes into the engine, its computer will adjust for this difference and add additional fuel—resulting in increased performance and speed.

Additional performance can also be gained by creating a less restrictive exhaust system. As with the air intake, if the vehicle's computer notes less exhaust, it will make adjustments and ask for more air and fuel to be cycled through the engine—again resulting in increased performance and speed.

OPTION ONE

The easiest performance upgrade is to replace your vehicle's air filter. Performance air filters are constructed of fabric and coated in a thin layer of oil. This combination allows more air to travel through them, while maintaining the ability to clean the air and protect the engine. Performance air filters are available for almost every application, allowing you to simply replace the paper air filter that your vehicle came with. As an added bonus, these filters are washable and reusable for hundreds of thousands of miles (a nice "green" benefit as well). This simple modification can yield a power increase of 5 percent or more.

OPTION TWO

For even more "go fast," many aftermarket companies offer replacement air intake systems for popular model vehicles. As with the performance air filter, a performance air intake system increases the amount of air available to the engine for even greater performance gains. This slightly more complicated modification can yield a power increase of 10 percent or more.

OPTION THREE

With your engine's improved ability to take in fresh air, the next logical increase can be gained through installing a less restrictive exhaust system. In most cases this means a performance muffler. For most, this will require a professional installation. It can yield a power increase of 15 percent or more.

So there you have it, three quick and painless options that can be used individually or in combination to make your ride faster!

-86-

IMPROVE GAS MILEAGE

CHAD KNAUS

> Chad Knaus is the NASCAR Sprint Cup crew
> chief for the #48 car currently driven by Jimmie Johnson,
> owned by Jeff Gordon, and operated by
> Hendrick Motorsports.

As our daily battle to conserve our planet's oil reserves continues, each one of us can do a little to help avoid the overconsumption of gasoline as well as help our own pockets in the process. Here are a few quick tips:

1. As simple as it sounds, keep your tires inflated. Roll a tire that is completely deflated and one that is properly inflated. The properly inflated tire will roll a lot easier than the flat one. So a direct result will be that your car will roll easier. And make sure your car has radial tires, as the sidewall of a radial tire is much stiffer and will roll easier than the softer sidewall of the bias ply tire.

2. Always keep your car tuned up and in proper running condition. Change your oil, oil filter, air filter, and spark plugs as per your manufacturer's recommendations. Using a synthetic oil will also help.

3. Driving style has an awful lot to do with whether or not you save fuel. You can help by letting off the throttle pedal early and easing onto the brakes when coming to stop signs and stoplights. Then, when you start moving, you need to be very easy on the throttle and accelerate slowly. Starting and stopping aggressively can burn a lot of fuel. Keeping a consistent throttle position will also help. This is why taking the highway will always produce better fuel mileage than city driving.

4. Another thing that you can do, though it may not be the most comfortable, is not running the air-conditioning. The extra load from the compressor will eat up fuel. So you say, "Okay. I will roll the windows down." Well, the problem with that is if you are going more than 30 to 40 miles per hour, you are hurting the fuel mileage by increasing the aerodynamic drag on the car. Speaking of aerodynamic drag, you should not use luggage racks or the cool-looking storage compartments that attach to the roof of your vehicle. They increase the drag on your vehicle and hurt your fuel mileage, too.

5. You can get better fuel mileage by lightening your load. Let's say you are a plumber and you have one of those big utility trucks with the tool boxes and equipment in the back. The lighter you make your ride, the easier it is to accelerate and decelerate. So plan out your jobs accordingly and leave the unnecessary equipment at home. Along those same lines, a smaller vehicle will typically save you fuel since lighter cars and trucks are easier to accelerate and decelerate.

6. The last tip I am going to give you is the most obvious but the least practiced: carpool and take public transportation. It really doesn't take a genius—or a NASCAR crew chief, for that matter—to figure out that fewer cars and trucks on the road will save fuel. I

know that having your own car and your own space is what you want, but think about this: 500 cars traveling 100 miles a week is 50,000 miles a week traveled. That's 3,333 gallons of fuel at 15 miles per gallon. Now, if you cut that in half so that 250 cars are traveling 100 miles a week, that is 25,000 miles a week traveled. That adds up to 1,666 gallons at 15 miles per gallon, which is quite a savings in both fuel and money.

Safe travels.

-87-

COMMUTE

DAVID RIZZO

David Rizzo, a.k.a. Dr. Roadmap, honed his traffic-beating
skills as an L.A. traffic reporter. He has written two books
and four hundred newspaper columns on the subject of
Commute Management.

Fortunately, you do not have to keep up with the Joneses in order to get from point A to point B quickly on the roadways. Navigating around traffic congestion involves using your brain, not your gas pedal.

BEFORE YOU START YOUR TRIP

1. LOOK UP THE DESTINATION ON A MAP. Studies show that those who develop a greater knowledge of available streets and highways along their route can gain a 10 percent time savings. Even for destinations you've visited before, like your place of work, it still pays to study a map. Make note of any streets that run parallel to the highways you routinely take. This helps identify faster pathways when a road closure forces you to detour.

2. CHECK ON PROPOSED ROAD CONSTRUCTION. Rather than end up surprised by a miles-long backup courtesy of a cornrow of orange cones, be sure to look for upcoming road closures in the local section of your city's newspaper.

3. CHECK TRAFFIC CONDITIONS. The importance of getting a heads-up cannot be stressed enough. Whether your preferred source of traffic information is radio, television, or the Internet, keep monitoring reports until you're ready to leave.

4. ADJUST TIME OF DEPARTURE WHEN NECESSARY. In one study, a shift in time of only twenty-one minutes reduced wasted time in traffic by up to 70 percent. Keep in mind that leaving later, as opposed to earlier, occasionally yields results.

ON THE ROAD

1. CONTINUOUSLY MONITOR TRAFFIC CONDITIONS. Forcing yourself to constantly listen to traffic reports will keep you out of trouble more often than not. Most motorists tune in only when they see brake lights; by then it's too late.

2. UNDER HEAVY TRAFFIC CONDITIONS, DRIVE IN, OR NEXT TO, THE SLOW LANE. If an accident occurs up ahead, you can exit first to avoid getting sucked into the ensuing logjam. Especially when traffic slows unexpectedly, slow-lane trawling puts you in a position to exit the freeway quickly to take an alternate route.

3. STAY TO THE RIGHT WHEN THE LANES GET TIGHT. In other words, when a lane is taken away, whether by construction cones, accident, or design, you'll usually end up farther ahead in the queue if you stay in the far right lane for as long as possible.

4. STAY OBSERVANT. Keep attuned to any change in the pace of traffic. Sudden swerving or stopping up ahead may signify that the time has come to exit the freeway.

MAXIMIZING ALTERNATE ROUTES

1. KNOW WHEN TO TAKE AN ALTERNATE ROUTE. If you encounter recurring congestion—such as the usual sticky spots—then stay on the freeway because all the easy alternates have already been discovered. On the other hand, if an incident occurs—such as a crash or debris in the roadway—then leave the freeway ASAP, as conditions will only get worse. If attending a sporting event or concert, alternate routes work especially well.

2. IDENTIFY WHERE TO GET BACK ON THE FREEWAY. Always add at least one on-ramp to where the reporter states the accident lies. Two arguments support this advice: (1) pinpointing the exact location of an accident often proves elusive; and (2) everyone else will rush toward the first on-ramp that allows access back onto the freeway.

3. DO NOT REPEATEDLY BOB ON AND OFF THE FREEWAY. Make your decision and stick to your guns.

SAVING TIME ON SURFACE STREETS

1. TIME THE LIGHTS. Make the "key" light—located at major intersections—and you should be able to whisk through the green lights at subsequent smaller intersections by staying at the speed limit, no faster.

2. STAY IN THE FAST LANE. On most four-lane roads (two lanes in each direction), the inside (a.k.a. number one, or fast) lane usually works best more often than not. The only exception lies with roads that do not have cutouts for left-hand-turn lanes.

3. STAY OBSERVANT. Never let your guard down when intent on making good time. Constantly check up ahead for buses, emergency vehicles, or heavy pedestrian traffic. Adjust your lane, or route, accordingly.

—88—
CHANGE A TIRE

BARBARA TERRY

Barbara Terry is an auto mechanic, race car driver, and the owner of Barbara Terry Racing. She is a spokesperson for eBay Motors, Goodyear, Gillette, Shell Oil, Rain-X, and Turtle Wax, and writes a regular auto advice column for The Houston Chronicle.

C hanging a tire is like riding a bicycle—once you do it you will never forget how. Armed with this skill you will no longer have to wait helplessly for assistance that may never arrive, and you'll be able to keep more money in your pocket.

SAFETY

Safety must be your top priority whenever working on and around your car. Park your car on a flat surface, engage the emergency brake, and make sure to turn your car off and remove the keys from the ignition. If you are broken down on the side of the road, use road safety devices on all four corners of your vehicle to alert oncoming traffic of your presence—thousands of drivers die every year as a result of not using proper road safety devices such as flares or reflective triangles with disabled cars. It is always a good idea to be overprepared, so I suggest putting wheel blocks/chucks on both sides of the three working tires. In addition, you may want to put on gloves and safety glasses before changing the tire.

JACKING UP YOUR CAR AND REMOVING THE LUG NUTS

Remove the jack and tire iron from your vehicle and, *before* jacking your car up, loosen each lug nut on the wheel holding your damaged tire. When loosening the lugs you may have to use a little force—or "elbow grease." Just loosen the lug nuts; do not totally remove them at this point.

Next, position the jack on the ground directly under your car's frame—you will need to refer to your owner's manual for the exact positioning of the jack. Most car jacks these days use a screw-type scissor jack, which means you simply turn the knob at the end of the jack using the provided metal hand crank. Raise the jack until it makes contact with the car's frame and continue raising the car with the jack until the flat tire is completely off the ground.

Now remove the lug nuts and put them in a safe place—losing your nuts before using them to secure the spare to the car is a rookie move. You will also want to place the flat tire under the car frame as an extra safety precaution in the unlikely event that the jack fails.

REPLACING THE FLAT WITH THE SPARE

Position the spare tire over your wheel studs and put the lug nuts onto the wheel. I recommend using your foot as a balancing device. First, tighten the lug nuts by hand until they feel snug, making sure that you have them precisely aligned on the studs. Now get the tire iron and use as much torque as you physically can to tighten them. Then carefully lower the jack to let your car down flush with the ground and see if you can tighten the lugs any further.

READY TO ROLL

Put the flat tire in the back of your vehicle and make your way to your local tire store. If you drive a compact car, your spare is likely a "doughnut" tire, which is designed to be driven at a maximum of 50 mph.

PREVENTION

You will be less likely to fall victim to a flat if you check the condition of your tires monthly and maintain them at their recommended air pressure. To determine the proper pressure, refer either to your car's driver's-side doorjamb or to your owner's manual. As an alternative, you can locate the make, model, and size of your tire on the tire's sidewall and call your local tire store for the proper "PSI"—pounds per square inch.

It is also wise to inspect your spare tire every couple of months to make sure it is good enough to use if pressed into duty. Last, have your tires rotated and high-speed-balanced every six months or 500 miles to assure their even tread wear, which will not only make them last longer but also provide you with the safest and smoothest ride possible.

-89-

FIND A PARKING SPOT

ERIK FEDER

Erik Feder is the author of The Feder Guide to Where to Park Your Car in Manhattan (and Where <u>Not</u> to Park It!) *paperback-book series. His website features a one-of-a-kind parking search engine that allows motorists to search for legal street parking and garages in major cities by date, time of day, and cross street.*

A ll of us who drive have been late for a dinner, meeting, concert, event, or any number of other appointments because we couldn't find a parking spot. While no one can guarantee an available parking space, you can increase your chances of getting a great spot fast.

Whenever possible, be prepared. Make it a point to know the parking regulations in the area you'll be visiting. This means knowing not only where you can park but also where you *can't* park. What an absolute waste it is to drive down a street looking for parking where it is never legal to park (NO PARKING ANYTIME, NO STANDING ANYTIME). When this happens you are wasting time, wasting gas, and becoming ever more frustrated as you inch forward only to see the traffic light turn red again. Traffic seems to appear when you are looking for a parking spot in a hurry, doesn't it? A far better plan is to make a short list of the places where you know you can park and make a beeline straight for those streets.

But what about when you are in a new place or have no idea about the parking regulations at your destination? For these cases, here are some tricks you can use to find that available parking spot the second it becomes available:

1. When it's not too cold, roll down your windows. You'll find parking spots faster when using your ears as well as your eyes.

2. Look/listen for the telltale sight/sound of keys jingling in someone's hand.

3. Try to spot someone walking near parked cars with shopping bags in hand.

4. Listen for the sound of a car alarm being disabled—you might also catch the flash of taillights when this happens.

5. Be aware of activity inside parked cars—windows rolling down, parents buckling in children, drivers fiddling with stereos. All are good signs that a car may be about to vacate your parking spot.

In the best-case scenario, you should be prepared with your short list of good places to park while paying attention for signs of someone about to leave. Start with small, one-block circles around your destination, and then make the circles a little bigger if necessary. Remember that a short walk is healthy, so don't be afraid to drift four or five blocks away from your starting point. You're better off continually circling than staying in one place; you can always return to where you started and repeat if necessary.

Perhaps most important: don't be afraid to try to find that parking space in the first place. People tell me all the time that it's impossible to find street parking in Manhattan. They are wrong. Recently, I was headed into Manhattan for a meeting. I made my short list of blocks where street parking would be legal, albeit difficult to find. I pulled up to a red light across from the first block where I would try to find parking. As the light turned green, I saw a man with keys in hand nearing a parked car. Sure enough, as I crossed the intersection he got in the car and started it up. I pulled up next to him and grabbed the spot when he left. I had a free and legal parking spot for the night. Total elapsed time spent looking for this spot: five seconds.

Was I lucky? Of course, but we make our own luck, don't we? Without my list, I wouldn't have been at that block at the right time. If I weren't paying attention, I would have missed my chance. Follow these guidelines and you'll save money and time while reducing your stress level.

FUTURE

–90–

STOP AGING IN ITS TRACKS

HENRY LODGE

Dr. Henry Lodge is an internist in Manhattan, where he heads a twenty-three-doctor practice. He is the coauthor of Younger Next Year *and* Younger Next Year for Women. *Lodge is a professor at Columbia University's College of Physicians and Surgeons.*

You are in charge of the rest of your life.

The biology of aging is becoming clearer every year, with science unlocking the keys to a dramatically longer and healthier life. Bad luck and random illness still count, but 70 percent of aging is optional; scientists can now double the healthy life spans of worms, mice, and fungus cells through genetic manipulation. The good news is that you can put yourself in the driver's seat and control the signals sent to every corner of your body by simply changing your daily lifestyle.

You speak to your body all the time, every day of your life. You tell your cells exactly what to do by the way you move, the way you eat, and the way you feel emotionally, all of which determine the signals sent to your brain, your heart, your joints . . . to every cell in your body. If you send the right signals, you can reverse the patterns of aging and live a vibrant, radically younger, and healthier life.

Though time is not on your side, I am, so let's get right to it. Here are the top ten rules for reclaiming your body and your youth:

1. EXERCISE six days a week. There's not a lot of wiggle room in this one, because exercise is one of nature's master control signals for your body.

2. PERFORM AEROBIC EXERCISE four days per week by using the machines at the gym, cycling, or taking brisk walks on the beach. Your circulatory system is your first line of defense against cancer, heart disease, strokes, and Alzheimer's. Moreover, aerobic exercise is emerging as a natural antidepressant—recent studies have found it to be just as powerful as Prozac, with no side effects.

3. STRENGTH TRAIN two days per week. Strength training signals your muscles and bones to grow denser and stronger. Even more important, strength-training repairs your joints. It keeps them from falling apart, and keeps you feeling and living younger.

4. QUIT EATING JUNK. Most people eat way too much junk food, and you know exactly what it is when you see it. Cut it out!

5. EAT LESS of everything.

6. EAT MORE SLOWLY, and do your best to enjoy your meals. Tons of research about successful weight loss points to the importance of portion control, and the only way to achieve this is to slow way, way down while you're eating.

7. SPEND LESS THAN YOU MAKE. Overwhelming financial burdens and the stress they create will rob you of your health, vitality, and youth.

8. CARE. Emotion is one of the most important determinants of physical health and quality of life. Caring about your life and the people around you, taking pride in what you do, and putting meaning back into the equation are biological imperatives.

9. CONNECT AND COMMIT. We are rapidly losing our sense of community just as science is revealing that human connection is a profoundly important determinant of long-term health outcomes, including cancer, heart attacks, strokes, Alzheimer's, and many other ills we used to think were driven purely by physical and genetic makeup. Get out there and rejoin your community, find old friends, and meet new ones.

10. HAVE FUN! Play is a biological godsend for mammals. If you've ever watched otters sliding down a riverbank, dolphins cavorting in the sea, or even a golden retriever running after a Frisbee, you've witnessed how deeply wired into our natures play is. Adult Americans have lost the knack for simply playing, and it's profoundly important to the rest of your life. So make it a priority to reconnect with your inner child.

Take back the reins of your biology by following these simple rules, and you'll quickly feel young and wonderful. With life spans rising so rapidly, you need to get ready for a long one.

-91-

QUIT SMOKING

YEFIM SHUBENTSOV

Yefim Shubentsov has been in private practice for more than twenty-seven years and has treated more than 134,000 clients. His treatment is designed to be effective after just one appointment.

If you want to quit smoking, follow these conditions:

1. Don't exaggerate the problem. Smoking is just a pleasure and nothing else. You don't feel any pain; you just miss it as kids miss candy. You are simply experiencing discomfort, especially after a meal or a drink.

2. Our brain is like a biological computer. It is necessary to give it straight directions. If you decide to do something, it will be simple and easy. But if you decide you will "do your best," it will be difficult or impossible because the best allows for two options—*yes* or *no*. *No* is easier. For example: You brush your teeth every day and if you forget to do it one morning you feel lousy the whole day long because we now consider it unacceptable not to brush our teeth every day. But a lot of people "try" to do exercises every morning and they drop it because they allow themselves to "try"

rather than commit to it. Essentially, they permit themselves to fail. The conclusion: Don't give your brain a chance to cheat.

3. No substitutes. Put nothing in your mouth instead of cigarettes, cigars, or pipes. All substitutes are your enemies. No gum, no straw, no toothpicks. Nothing. All of this stuff serves as a reminder. If you want to forget something, don't remind yourself of it. If you break up with somebody and keep that person's pictures and souvenirs, they will just remind you of how good it used to be.

4. Don't use nicotine supplies (e.g., the patch or gum). Medical statistics say that in three days (seventy-two hours) the human body clears out all nicotine. If you try to stop smoking and are off cigarettes for three days, the first cigarette on the fourth day will make you dizzy. In other words, your reaction to the first cigarette you ever had in your life and the first cigarette you have after three days of not smoking will be the same. So why would you need a patch for two months if after three days you are free of nicotine?

5. Don't dwell on your problem. This is the most important point. If smoking comes to your mind, immediately change the subject. One day an eighty-one-year-old gentleman came to my office and told me he began to smoke when he was seven years old. "I adore smoking and I don't want to stop. I don't want to be here but my cardiologist told me that it is my last year if I keep smoking. I smoke five and a half packs a day."

In six months he came back and said, "You saved my life." When he returned home that first day he realized that he had been without cigarettes for eight hours. It was a shock to him. But he was afraid of future temptations so he took my advice—to change the subject. He began to write down names of old girlfriends, but he had forgotten many so he went to a store and bought a map. He wrote down whom he had met in each city. It took six months to write his love history. While you don't need to count your romances, follow his lead and change the subject immediately. Don't let it become an obsession.

HOW DO YOU AVOID GAINING EXTRA WEIGHT WHEN YOU STOP SMOKING?

Put nothing in your mouth between meals: no gum, no snacks, no juice, no diet soda—nothing! Only water if you are thirsty because water has no taste. Your brain "tells" your hands to put something in your mouth automatically. Like all "automatic" problems, this problem will be active for approximately ten days. If you had a stick shift car and you exchanged it for an automatic, your hands would search for the clutch for about ten days. Without this "automatic memory" you would have to learn how to drive the car from scratch every morning.

Similarly, if you put food in your mouth instead of a cigarette even once, you create a monster. You used to smoke, now you will eat. One cigarette equals one snack; one hundred cigarettes equal one hundred snacks. Imagine how you will look! Eat three meals a day and nothing in between. In ten days your automatic memory will be erased.

—92—

GET IN SHAPE

GUNNAR PETERSON

A personal trainer who works with many celebrities and professional athletes, Gunnar Peterson is the author of G-Force, the creator of the Core Secrets workout series, and the developer of a number of health and fitness products.

If you work through the following ten tips consistently, you will come closer to your fitness goals in less time than if you employ them only sporadically. You will also be making the most out of your time, which will in turn get you there faster.

1. Decide where you want to be physically (e.g., have reduced body fat, have greater energy reserves, or just look better when you're nuded up!). Don't waiver, don't be shy. Decide and then own it.

2. Take a realistic look at your schedule and figure out where you can make time for exercise. If you have been sedentary, start working out two times per week and work your way up to more. No matter what your schedule looks like, you do have time. There are people who are busier and more exhausted than you who get their workouts in. And remember to take at least one day off per week; on the seventh day, even He rested.

3. Commit to your decision to make the necessary changes (exercise; food; drink—hydration, that is; and sleep). On a regular basis you don't have to be doing 100 percent; just keep working at it and let nothing come between you and your health and well-being. Less on some days is fine; every climb has flats. Remember, improved overall quality of life is what this is all about; your improved physique is merely a by-product, a bonus.

4. Recognize that resistance training (weights) is as integral to changing your body as cardio (aerobic work), flexibility (stretching), and functional training (real-life movements built into your training routines). Don't try to fool your body; there are no shortcuts, only smart cuts.

5. Find a place that is close to home, close to work, or in your home where you can work out. The best gym or class, if it is out of the way, will end up being the worst. Any location in the home where you will be interrupted multiple times per workout is not ideal.

6. Contrary to popular belief, you don't have to announce your new goals to friends and family. Just get started.

7. Do not set a "date" to get started. There is no such thing as a "getting-in-shape anniversary," just like there is no such thing as an "exercise anniversary." This applies to starting your program in the first place as well as restarting it when you miss a day or two. Don't start "on Monday" or "after your vacation" or "once the kids go back to school." Start now.

8. Even if you can't complete whatever you planned to do, do something, however little, instead of doing nothing or instead of planning on doubling down in your next workout—because you won't. It's the only way to stay consistent, which, in turn, is the only way to reach your goals faster.

9. Give yourself credit for what you do, and don't beat yourself up for what you don't do. This applies to the exercise portion of your program as well as the nutrition part. Self-encouragement is a major contributor to keeping you on your path, which means reaching your goals faster.

10. Have fun. Learn to enjoy the process. If you approach exercise with dread, or if you focus only on what it is doing "for you," it will seem interminable. If you let go and actually teach and allow yourself to enjoy it, you will reach your goals faster. You will also stick with your program longer, which means you will surpass whatever goals you set at the beginning and you will be better than even you could have imagined. Take that to the bank.

I hope you apply what I have shared with you—I wish someone had laid this out for me when I was a fat kid trying to get my groove on.

—93—
SPEED UP YOUR METABOLISM

MARK HYMAN

Dr. Mark Hyman is editor in chief of Alternative Therapies in Health and Medicine, *the premier peer-reviewed journal in the field of integrative and alternative medicine. He is the author of six books, including* Ultrametabolism: The Simple Plan for Automatic Weight Loss. *He was the co-medical director at Canyon Ranch in Lenox, Massachusetts.*

Most of us believe we are stuck with the metabolism we were born with—it's either fast or slow and there's nothing we can do about it. Thankfully, new scientific discoveries prove this is not true. Anybody, at any time, can almost instantly reboot his or her metabolism.

Your body runs according to the laws of nature. Adhere to those laws and your body will thank you and your metabolism and your health will dramatically improve. Ignore those laws and you will gain weight and experience a slow but progressive decline in your health and well-being.

Follow these basic laws that govern metabolism and health and you will see immediate and long-lasting results:

1. Rid your diet of toxic foods, which block metabolism. These include high-fructose corn syrup, trans fats (also known as hydrogenated fats), and all processed foods with ingredients that come from a food chemist's lab and not a farmer's field. If you don't recognize any ingredient on the label, or it is not from a whole, real food, put it back on the shelf.

2. Eat organic. Pesticides, hormones, and antibiotics in food all slow down metabolism.

3. Eat whole, real foods, mostly from plants. This is what our bodies were designed to thrive on—vegetables, fruit, whole grains, beans, nuts, seeds, and lean animal protein such as eggs, chicken, and fish.

4. Get rid of inflammatory food from your diet. A large percentage of people have developed low-grade food sensitivities that promote inflammation and slow down metabolism. Try a week without gluten (wheat, barley, rye, oats, spelt, Kamut) and dairy and see what happens. If you lose a lot of weight and feel better, then leave them out of your diet.

5. Keep your blood sugar even by avoiding sugar and flour products, which are the biggest factors slowing your metabolism.

6. Eat breakfast early in your day and eat protein with each meal. Having protein for breakfast is critical to jump-start your metabolism for the day and prevent overeating later on; eat eggs, nuts or nut butters, a protein shake, or even leftovers from the night before.

7. Eat often. Your metabolism runs faster with a slow, steady source of fuel. Be sure to have three meals and a couple of snacks.

8. Finish your entire food intake for the day at least two to three hours before going to bed. If you sleep with food in your stomach you will store it, not burn it.

9. Get seven to eight hours of sleep a night. Sleep deprivation triggers high levels of grehlin, the hunger hormone driving you to crave and eat more sugar and refined carbohydrates.

10. Exercise intelligently. Incorporate interval training (going at 90 to 95 percent of your peak heart rate for thirty to sixty seconds, followed by three to five minutes at 60 to 65 percent of your peak heart rate, for a total of thirty minutes) into your exercise program two to three days a week. You will then burn more calories all day and while you sleep.

11. Build muscle. This is where your metabolism lives. Your biggest metabolic engine is your muscle mass. Use it or lose it. Yoga, weights, exercise bands, or machines all keep your muscle from wasting away.

12. Take a multivitamin daily. Vitamins and minerals are the helpers that keep your metabolism running. Think of them as oil that greases the wheels of your metabolic engine.

13. Take a fish-oil supplement daily. Omega-3 fats are essential for your cells to run properly; they help balance your blood sugar and speed up your metabolism.

–94–

LOSE WEIGHT

HARLEY PASTERNAK

Harley Pasternak is a trainer who has worked with celebrities such as Jessica Simpson, Halle Berry, and Alicia Keys. He is the author of two books, including The 5 Factor Diet.

I love it when a pilot talks about making up time in the air after a late departure. You might think he'll just fly faster, but that isn't the case. Flying faster eats up the engine's fuel and is often unsafe. Rather, the pilot uses science and a good plan to chart a better course.

Weight loss can be approached the same way. Whether you want to lose ten or fifty pounds, you can't cheat the number, but you can cheat the system.

Contrary to the plan most dieters follow (starving themselves), I want you eating five times a day. Don't calorie-count or weigh your food. Instead, think of your body as a furnace that needs to be stoked regularly to stay burning hot. Food is the fuel that keeps your fire ablaze. Each meal will hit five key criteria: a healthy fat; a low glycemic index carb ("GI" is, simply put, the rate at which foods are digested), like wild rice, beans, or veggies; protein, like chicken, seafood, or cottage cheese; fiber; and a nonsugar beverage. This will keep your metabolism revving, which is key to avoiding a drop in your blood sugar and entering the dreaded fat-storing zone.

A sample day might begin with a bowl of high-fiber cereal and nonfat milk and a slice of multigrain toast. Skip the juice bar (OJ is too high in sugar) and head for a cup of tea instead. For your midmorning snack, try a cup of lowfat cottage cheese with blueberries. If cottage cheese isn't to your liking, try some apple slices with peanut butter blended with nonfat yogurt, as a dip. For lunch, pick a protein like grilled chicken breast. Put it over romaine lettuce (it's packed with calcium) and add some corn, black beans, nonfat shredded cheese, and your favorite veggies. Top it with salsa and crunched up flaxseed tortillas for a delicious taco salad. As an afternoon snack, try roasted red pepper hummus and multigrain crackers. It's a breeze to mix up. Toss chickpeas, a splash of olive oil, roasted red peppers, and lemon juice in a blender and you have homemade hummus. For dinner, keep it simple. One of my favorite quick fixes is a whole wheat tortilla baked with tomato sauce, nonfat ricotta cheese, sundried tomatoes, and shredded mozzarella. Each of these snacks and meals takes less than five minutes to prepare and is both delicious and totally healthy.

Now that we have you eating properly, cheat. Yes, you read that right. I want you to cheat one day a week. And when I say cheat, I mean it. Some of my clients like to cheat for all three meals, while others, like me, prefer to cheat for just one meal. I save my "cheat" for Sunday brunch. Not only is it a treat that I look forward to each week but it also serves an important purpose. Cheating like this keeps your metabolism guessing so it keeps working hard for you.

But cheat only once a week. Cheating here and there will lead to counterproductive results.

Exercise is an essential part of your plan. Getting active serves two purposes: it helps you shed unwanted pounds more quickly, and it gets you to your optimum health level. You need to get your heart rate up and your cardiovascular muscles working to ensure that you are doing all you can to be healthy. As you follow your eating and workout plan, chart your course through a journal. Think of the journal as your personal flight log to ensure that you stay the course and reach your goal ahead of schedule. Now, if we can just get the airlines to be as efficient as your new lifestyle, we'll all have a little less stress in our lives.

-95-

REDUCE DEBT

JENNIFER OPENSHAW

Jennifer Openshaw is president of WeSeed. She is the author of The Millionaire Zone, AOL's *family finance editor, and host of ABC Radio's* Winning Advice.

B ad debt happens to good people—whether from a job loss, a marriage ending, or a medical crisis. The average household carries about nine thousand dollars in credit card debt. Ouch! If you're trying to get out from under, read these six serious moves.

1. 15 MINUTES TO CUT THE "FAT" AND AVOID THE TRAP

We're all guilty of spending on things we don't need. Take a look at last month's credit card and bank statements and identify where your money is going. Add up all the things you didn't need—dinners out, CDs, expensive gifts to impress people—and chances are you'll be able to find a couple of hundred dollars to devote to paying off your debts.

Remember, the credit card companies make billions by keeping you in what I call the "Minimum Payment Trap." So, your goal is to help rein in your spending and beef up those monthly payments (unless you have serious debt, in which case we'll explore other options). A case in point: if you owed $30,000 in credit card debt and made only minimum payments, it would take you forty-five years to pay it off and cost nearly $60,000 in interest— assuming you don't charge anything else.

2. RANK, ROLL, AND SAVE!

Rank your top five biggest expenditures and see what you can do to save big bucks. Examples:

- For your home, consider refinancing or getting a renter.
- Get rid of the extra car; turn it in for something that you can pay outright that will also save you on insurance and gas. Also, avoid making multiple trips during the day, which wastes gas and your precious time.
- If you're footing your medical bills, tell the doctor's office and ask what they can do to lower payments or provide better terms. Doctors would rather get paid than not, so they're likely to work with you.
- To lower food costs, enjoy potluck dinners with friends and use loyalty rewards programs.

3. DON'T DELAY; PAY TODAY

When you get the mail and tuck that bill away, you create more stress for yourself and increase the chances of a late payment. And those late payments will end up dinging your credit. Worse: You used to have thirty days to make your payments, and now it can be as short as two weeks. And finally, credit card companies often increase your interest rate once you're late.

So eliminate the worry and make the payment once the bill arrives.

4. TO CONSOLIDATE, NOT ALWAYS GREAT

Debt consolidation usually involves getting a loan to pay off your debts. But if you're in dire straights, you'll need more drastic measures. Many people discover that because of their credit history, a loan is simply out of the question. And if you own your home, you need to ask if getting a loan is a wise move.

A consolidation loan is just a transfer of debt in which you're trading in unsecured debt (the credit card debt) for debt now secured by your home. While you may lower your interest rate considerably, does it make sense to put your home at risk if there's a chance you won't be able to make the payments? Studies show that most people who borrow from their home or otherwise consolidate to pay off their debt simply go back into debt. Also, watch for fees, one of the biggest traps of any loan. You don't want to spend thousands on a consolidation loan if you plan to sell your home in the next year or two.

Borrowing from your home is generally best when you're using the equity to make additional smart investments that will build your wealth.

5. NEGOTIATE, IF IT'S NOT TOO LATE

When a debt settlement company gets involved, they negotiate better rates and payment terms with your creditors on your behalf. Debt settlement, also known as debt negotiation, is an option for those people with legitimate debt problems who might otherwise face bankruptcy—such as the person who has lost a job or has had a medical crisis that is now depleting his or her savings.

You need to be cautious and understand the risks involved with debt settlement. If you're considering this option, watch out for the following:

- Failure to tell you how your credit report will be impacted
- High upfront fees before work is performed
- Promises that your creditors won't be contacting you

6. TALK, DON'T HIDE

Finally, about the worst thing you can do if you're dealing with debt—or, rather, hiding from it—is to pretend it's not there.

Your first move is to start talking to your creditors. If you're having trouble making payments, they'll almost always work with you and will allow a delayed payment without it hurting your credit report.

New laws have made it tougher to file bankruptcy and get a "fresh start." The laws now require that anyone with an income over the state's average be required to pay back some of their debt, which means you're not able to "wipe the slate clean" as easily as you could in the past. You'll also have to work with an attorney, which will cost you. Finally, bankruptcy can have terrible consequences— from additional stress to failing to get the job you wanted because your prospective employer took a look at your credit report.

If you're facing debt, take action. Your future is too important not to.

—96—

GET A LOAN

SIR RICHARD BRANSON

> Sir Richard Branson is the founder and president of the
> Virgin Group, parent company of Virgin Money USA, a
> business that manages loans between friends and family
> members. As a young entrepreneur, he got a loan from an
> aunt that helped launch his music empire.

When I first started out in the record business and was struggling to get by, I asked my family for help because I didn't fit my bank's requirements for a business loan. Banks and credit card companies tend to fund or reject loan requests based on the 5 Cs of credit:

- Your **capacity** to repay
- **Capital** you put in yourself
- **Collateral** available in case you don't pay
- **Conditions** your business will face
- Your **character**—as they see it

Needless to say, people who don't meet the criteria (or aren't getting a good interest rate) often turn to family and friends for quick loans, which are typically less costly and more flexible. It's something people have done for ages to launch a business, pay for college, buy a house, or pay off high-interest credit card debt. It worked for me, and it's worked for other successful entrepreneurs like Sam Walton, the founder of Wal-Mart, who borrowed $20,000 from his father-in-law to buy his first retail store, and Leslie Wexner, who opened the women's clothing store The Limited with a $5,000 loan from his aunt. It might be just the thing for you, too.

Of course, putting a loved one's money and your relationship at risk might not be something you want to do. But by following a few simple guidelines, borrowing from people you know can be a simpler, faster, more flexible, and often more affordable way to secure a loan and pursue your dream.

So let's get started. Here it is in three steps:

1. FIND SOMEONE WHO AGREES TO GIVE YOU THE LOAN. Consider *any* person in your circle of relatives and friends that will understand and support what you're trying to accomplish.

2. DOCUMENT THE DEBT. Sealing the agreement with a kiss, a handshake, or a cocktail-napkin IOU is a recipe for trouble. Do it right (and protect your relationship) by using a proper promissory note and repayment plan.

3. PAY IT BACK. Make payments on time, keep accurate records of the loan and its repayment, and provide year-end reports to your lender (or ask a professional to do these things for you).

Simple, right? Yes, in theory. But because asking for (and receiving) a loan from those close to you can be fraught with relationship pitfalls and emotional stresses, keep the following additional tips in mind:

ASK FROM THE HEART

"Um . . . hey . . . I was wondering . . ." Asking for a loan can be an awkward conversation—but it doesn't have to be. Prepare to speak from the heart about what you wish to do and what you need to get there. Regardless of how you ask, be yourself, tell the truth, and, by all means, don't ask someone who can't afford to help.

HAVE A PLAN AND FOLLOW THROUGH

Once you've got a commitment for a loan, your lender may well have two questions in mind:

- Will I ever see my money again?
- Will the loan hurt our relationship?

Family and friends are precious, so have a plan for how you're going to repay the loan. And then by all means stick with it. That will erase any doubts about your commitment to repay the loan. Your lender wants you to succeed and will likely be more flexible than a bank to accommodate any misfortunes, as long as you are really trying.

–97–

BUILD WEALTH

SHARON EPPERSON

Sharon Epperson is a personal finance correspondent for CNBC. She is the author of The Big Payoff: 8 Steps Couples Can Take to Make the Most of Their Money— and Live Richly Ever After *and a personal finance columnist for* USA Weekend *magazine.*

T o build wealth quickly and effectively, you need to define your financial goals—and stick to them! If you don't have a road map, now is the time to make one. Be both specific and realistic. Do you need a five-bedroom, three-bathroom Colonial, or would a three-bedroom townhouse serve your needs? Are you expecting a child and hoping to figure out a way to work only part-time? Do you want to retire early or late? Ask yourself: What do I want my money to do for me?

Whatever your aspirations, you cannot build wealth quickly without making sure your finances are in order first. Start by getting any debilitating debt under control. Next, establish a cushion of cash that you can access quickly in case of an emergency—e.g., losing your job, getting sick, or suddenly having to replace the hot water heater in your house. Tapping your long-term investments for such purposes can set you back years. So establish a sufficient emergency fund (to cover at least three to six months of expenses). With that taken care of, it's time to put your money to work.

Begin systematically stashing more money away by contributing to several different savings pots simultaneously. Take maximum advantage of tax-deferred savings vehicles. A good place to start is your employer's retirement savings program, including 401(k) plans. Automatic payroll deducations make this the simplest way to start saving. You should try to contribute the maximum amount that your employer and federal law will allow. If your company offers a matching program (contributing money to your account based on the amount of money that you put in), contribute at least to that threshold. It's free money for your nest egg.

How much money should you put away? Whatever you're saving now, try to add a little more. For a thirty-five-year-old, investing an additional $50 a week in a tax deferred account can result in an extra $265,000 for retirement by age sixty-five, assuming a reasonable 7 percent annual rate of return on the investment.

If your income qualifies, you should also fully fund a Roth IRA. Since income limits on a Roth IRA are higher than for a traditional, deductible IRA, it's a better option for many people. Unlike 401(k) and traditional IRA contributions, payments into a Roth account must be made on an after-tax basis—but when you withdraw the money at retirement, you don't pay any tax. (You'll be able to convert the traditional IRA to a Roth IRA, regardless of income, in 2010.) A big bonus: contributions to a Roth are yours to take out when you want to without penalty—so this account can double as an emergency reserve.

When you've maxed out all tax-advantaged options, set aside money in a taxable investment account and, again, fund it as regularly as possible.

Not sure what stock or bond mutual funds to invest in? Seek out a local financial adviser and ask for his or her advice on asset allocation. You don't have to be rich to get a professional to map out a plan that includes the appropriate mix of stocks, bonds, and other investments (perhaps real estate and commodities, too) that will help you become a millionaire.

Now that you're saving like a pro, make sure you have the mindset to match; you don't want to veer off plan impetuously based on short-term results. So don't worry if you see the major stock market averages plunge 10 percent in two weeks. Most likely your goal is to use those funds for retirement ten, twenty, or thirty years from now. And stop panicking about the value of your home sliding 8 percent in the past year. You bought the home to have extra room for your growing family, not simply as an investment.

You may believe it's impossible to save any more than you currently are and still keep up with your bills. But the sooner you start to save, the longer you'll do it, the faster you'll build wealth, and the bigger the payoff will be.

-98-

MAKE LIFE CHANGES

ALAN DEUTSCHMAN

Alan Deutschman is a former business journalist turned consultant and the author of three books, including Change or Die: The Three Keys to Change at Work and in Life. *He is the executive director of Unboundary, a strategy consulting firm for corporate executives.*

Conventional wisdom holds that people rarely succeed at efforts to change the deep-rooted patterns of how they think, feel, and act. A study by psychologists at the University of Minnesota found that 80 percent of people break their New Year's resolutions by mid-February—or conveniently "forget" having made them in the first place. Even when faced with life-threatening crises, people still struggle to change: two years after undergoing coronary bypass surgery, 90 percent of heart patients haven't been able to maintain a healthier lifestyle and reduce the stress that could kill them.

The problem isn't that we can't change—neuroscientists find the brain's "plasticity" astonishing and find people to be capable of tackling complex new learning at any age. The problem is that most of us approach change in the wrong ways. But by applying proven ideas from psychology, personal transformations can be dramatic—and surprisingly fast:

1. START WITH BIG CHANGES, NOT SMALL ONES. One of the keys to making changes stick is realizing clear, tangible benefits within a short time—usually no longer than a month. Change can be difficult, frustrating, even humiliating, but if you can clearly see positive results, you're more likely to find sacrifices to be worthwhile—and stick with them. As a result, it's usually easier and faster for people to make big, sweeping changes than small, incremental ones. If you start eating brown rice, tofu, and steamed vegetables every day, you'll surely miss the greasy pleasures of cheeseburgers and fries, but the ten pounds you lose after only one month will make you feel so much better that you'll stock up on more brown rice. In contrast, if you switch from cheeseburgers to hamburgers, you'll still feel deprived, but you won't notice any significant change in how you feel—and you'll probably start adding back that slice of Cheddar again before long.

2. ACT "AS IF." When trying to make a big change, you'll feel like an impostor at first. Even if you manage to drag yourself to the jogging path at dawn, you'll think the other people running around are the real athletes while you're just a fraud. You'll still *feel* like a hopeless couch potato rather than a jock. The trick to overcoming this roadblock is to act "as if" you're the kind of person you're trying to become. Eventually, your new behavior will feel natural. Until then, pretend you're an actor in a real-life stage drama.

3. "REFRAME" THE SITUATION. We often struggle to change because our minds become locked in our old way of thinking. So sometimes we need new metaphors to help us see possibilities in a new light—and to help us preserve our vital self-respect as

we reckon courageously with our past troubles. For example, Caroline Knapp, author of the candid memoir *Drinking: A Love Story*, was aided in her recovery from alcoholism when she came to view her new, sober life as a "divorce" from her tumultuous twenty-year "love affair" with drinking, as though she had finally escaped from the pull of an incredibly seductive man who was wrong for her. The new metaphor enabled Knapp to view her previous life as a romantic adventure rather than solely a source of regrets.

4. DON'T DO IT ALONE. We live in a culture that celebrates self-reliance. We believe we can do anything on our own if only we try harder and work longer, and that change is simply a matter of summoning the willpower. We cling to these ideas even when we've tried again and again to make a life change, each failed attempt met with growing hopelessness. It is time to set aside these beliefs: decades of psychological research proves that the key to personal change is forming a close, emotional relationship with another person or group of peers. So go out, find people who embody the characteristics you want to achieve, and connect with them. We all need coaches, mentors, and role models. They possess the skills we must learn and the mind-sets we must adopt, and can provide the encouragement we need to accomplish our goals. Through their own personal examples they inspire our belief in ourselves and our expectation that we can make changes we previously thought impossible.

-99-

GO GREEN

GRAHAM HILL

Graham Hill is vice president of Interactive at Discovery Communications, home of the Planet Green channel. He is founder of TreeHugger.com, the Web's most-visited green lifestyle and news site. Hill is coauthor of Ready, Set, Green: Eight Weeks to Modern Eco-Living.

You don't have to install solar panels on your roof or buy a hybrid car to go green. In fact, going green fast is actually easy and inexpensive because at its core green living is all about efficiency, simplicity, and healthfulness.

The three basic tenets of green living are reduce, reuse, and recycle. So the first step in going green is to simply cut back on the amount of stuff you buy and use. Whether it's electricity or paper clips, consuming less is the most effective way to lighten your impact. Of course we all need to buy things sometimes, so consuming wisely—choosing goods that last and taking everything home in a reusable bag, for instance—is a must. And when an item has reached the end of its useful life, it should be properly disposed of or, ideally, donated or recycled.

For most people, our homes and transportation choices are the biggest sources of our carbon dioxide emissions, the main gas associated with global warming. So being more energy efficient around the house and on the road should top your to-do list. The following tips suggest the easiest and most effective actions you can take to reach these objectives quickly without sacrificing your time, money, or comfort:

AROUND THE HOUSE:

- Turn off lights when you leave a room. Replace incandescent bulbs with compact fluorescent lights (CFLs), which use 75 percent less energy and last roughly ten times as long. Target high-use areas such as kitchens and porches.

- Unplug cell phone, MP3 player, and other gadget chargers, which draw electricity even when the electronics they power are fully charged or disconnected. Or place gadgets and other appliances that use standby energy on a power strip, which can be turned off without unplugging everything individually.

- Turn the thermostat up two degrees in summer and down two degrees in winter.

- Many utility companies offer a green energy option for a nominal fee. If yours does, sign up. While the energy delivered won't come directly from green sources, you'll be supporting clean energy projects.

- Using the dishwasher is actually more efficient than washing by hand, but be sure to run yours only when full. The same goes for the washing machine, where you should launder clothes in cold water.

- Turn off the water while you brush your teeth or shave.

- Recycle. Many, if not most, municipalities accept aluminum, paper, glass, and certain plastics.

- Switch to nontoxic cleaning products, which will improve indoor air quality and are gentler on water going down the drain.

ON THE GO:

- Walk, ride a bike, or use public transportation whenever possible.

- Keep vehicles well maintained. Underinflated tires and dirty air-intake filters can significantly reduce gas mileage.

- Shut off your engine when running into the convenience store, waiting to pick up the kids at school, and in other similar situations.

- Fly direct whenever possible, which uses less fuel. Better yet, fly less altogether.

- Use a reusable coffee mug and water bottle.

AT THE STORE:

- Stash a reusable bag in your car, purse, or briefcase for carrying home groceries and other purchased goods.

- Avoid one-time-use products such as disposable cameras, plastic cups, and throwaway containers.

- Purchase products with the least amount of packaging.

- Choose local, organic, and minimally processed foods.

IN THE OFFICE:

- Shut down your computer at night.
- Sign up for paperless billing.
- Defend yourself against junk mail by visiting the Direct Marketing Association's website (www.dmachoice.org).
- Choose paper products made from a high percentage of post-consumer-recycled content, and use them conservatively; think twice before printing out e-mails; circulate memos digitally; and set printers to make double-sided copies.

One last tip: think of environmentalism as a universal sentiment, not an elitist club. After all, who doesn't want clean beaches, a healthy home, and nutritious food? Whether you try to accomplish three things on this list in three weeks or all of them in one day, it's important to set attainable goals. Once you meet them, set some more. Going green is an ongoing process, but getting started is as easy as the flick of a switch

–100–

MIND YOUR MANNERS IN A FAST-PACED WORLD

THOMAS P. FARLEY

Thomas P. Farley is the editor of the "Social Graces"
column in Town & Country *magazine. He is also*
the editor of Town & Country's Modern Manners:
The Thinking Person's Guide to Social Graces.

ushers of technology are forever promising that the latest gadget will buy us the time and happiness we crave. But such pledges are hollow. We've saved so many hours of television shows on our digital recorders that we need to set aside a night just to delete those we (grudgingly) come to realize we'll never watch. In place of handwritten thank-you notes we send text messages: "BTW, thx 4 dinr!"

As we multitask, we leave no time for recharging our *selves*. We take phone calls from the office while we're on vacation. We bring our laptops to bed to work on spreadsheets. We answer text messages during our sons' baseball games. With all of this busy work going on, is it any wonder we have less time (or inclination) for pleasantries? We've become too rushed to bother with man ners, those wonderful niceties that grease the wheels of social interaction.

The following are five things you can do right now to get off the tech treadmill and reclaim your manners:

1. PUT IT IN WRITING. *Hand*writing, that is. E-mailed thank-you notes are better than nothing, but the gold standard in gratitude remains a message that is well crafted, penned, and dropped in the mail. If you keep some stationery on hand, the whole process should take no more than five minutes. Not a bad time investment for something that will be appreciated and (often) saved for years to come.

2. HOLD THAT THOUGHT. Never take or make a phone call in the following places or situations:

- Urinal/bathroom stall
- Movie theater
- House of worship
- Funeral home
- Golf/tennis tournament
- Your year-end review
- Elevator
- Best man's toast
- Before, during, or after intercourse

If you're in the presence of others in a scenario not noted above and receive a phone call that you simply must take, politely excuse yourself and retire to somewhere out of earshot. No one wants to be held hostage to your conversation. Better yet, turn off your phone and live in the moment.

3. EXERCISE CARE WITH COLON-PAREN COMBOS. Unless you're a fourteen-year-old girl, do not flood your e-mails, IMs, or text messages with smileys, frownies, or other facial expressions. However, I'm a big believer that the smart use of emoticons can actually add nuance and irony to an e-mail. It can also go a long way toward avoiding misunderstandings or hurt feelings. Warning: Limit yourself to one or two emoticons per message. When your meaning requires more finessing than that, just pick up the phone.

4. PAY ATTENTION, PLEASE. If you're simultaneously watching *Oprah,* doing your taxes, and polishing off a pint of mint-chocolate-chip ice cream, don't choose now as the time to call your best friend. Chances are she'd much prefer your full attention as she relates the tale of last night's date. Turn off the TV, finish your taxes, and only then hit her number on speed dial. Give her your full self and she is sure to pay you back when the time comes when *you* want to talk.

5. TECH IS A LUXURY, NOT AN INALIENABLE RIGHT. It's amazing how quickly we come to view certain advances as sine qua non rather than guilty pleasures. On a recent flight I sat across from a man who had a conniption when the pretakeoff safety announcement preempted the football game he was watching on his seat back. Perish the thought that he miss a fumble for the sake of knowing what to do if he had to evacuate a burning aircraft. The same goes for those parents who—believing they need to be able to reach their child at any time of day—protest cell phone bans in classrooms. When I was in grade school I had to find a *dime* if I wanted to contact my mom. And if my parents needed me urgently, they simply called the school office. Somehow, I turned out okay.

ACKNOWLEDGMENTS

Five years, four *Experts' Guides*, and two babies later, this series could never have come to fruition without the help, support, and love of so many people.

My heartfelt thanks goes to the community of expert contributors, now over four hundred strong, who represent a blend of passion, charisma, and talent.

Special thanks go to: my brother, Tim Ettus. This book is so much better because of your input and editing talent. I will need to find a new excuse to talk to you every day. My editor, Aliza Fogelson, whose talent and sharp eye for detail are invaluable and to Sarah Breivogel, Donna Passannante, and the entire team at Clarkson Potter. Thank you for making beautiful books. My agent and friend, Jennifer Joel. Thank you for your magic. And to the effervescent Niki Castle. My illustrator and dear friend, Cathy Ross. Collaborating with you since sixth grade has been a source of huge joy. My friend-turned-attorney and great friend, David Baum. My wonderful publicist, Grace McQuade.

Thanks for your creative input: Liz Biber, Stefan C. Friedman, Tory Johnson, Jesse Kornbluth, Jennifer Prather, and Jessica Schell—your imprint is felt throughout this book.

My trusted professional friends: Dan Fannon, Dana Fulmore, Joanne Jones, Juda Kallus, Barbara Landreth, Josh Lipshutz, Sonya McPherson, and Matt Meyer.

Thanks to my devoted mom and dad for launching me with such a busy life that it required me to do this book to figure it all out. To Courtney, for becoming such an important part of my life. To Elaine and Dennis Leanse, the Fleischrons of Madison, the Bermans of Maui and the Habermans of East End for helping still be supportive and loving family.

Thanks to some of my favorite people who have inspired, advised, and supported me and this book series: Lenore and Maurice Ades, Alison Brod, David and Michaela Clary, Elissa Doyle, Beth Ferguson, Amy Fierstein, Rachel and Erik Geisler, Risa Goldberg, Jonathan Groberg, Meredith Kopit, Jason Levien, Jonathan Levine, Sarah Levy, Darcy Miller, Adam Nash, Valerie Neustadt, Amy Palmer, Erica Payne, Devon Pike, Manny Robinson, Josh Shaw, Lara Sivin, Amy Slothower, Gila Steinbock, Lucy Wohltman, and Bryn Zeckhauser.

My mommy friends, thanks for making the balancing act easier: Julie Brown, Jill Chodosch, Lee Klausner, Melissa Shaw, and Allison Udis.

Gratefully,
Samantha

EXPERTS' WEBSITES

Ablow, Keith	Overcome Guilt	www.livingthetruth.com
Arnot, Bob	Pick Up a Foreign Language	www.expertsmedia.com
Atkins, Dale	Bury the Hatchet	www.drdaleatkins.com
Baker, Dan	Get in a Good Mood	www.expertsmedia.com
Benjamin, Arthur	Do Math in Your Head	www.math.hmc.edu/~benjamin
Berg, Howard Stephen	Read and Comprehend	www.mrreader.com
Berman, Laura	Achieve Female Orgasm	www.drlauraberman.com
Bolles, Richard	Find Your Calling	www.jobhuntersbible.com
Bond, Marybeth	Navigate a New City	www.gutsytraveler.com
Boothman, Nicholas	Make Yourself Memorable	www.nicholasboothman.com
Branson, Richard	Get a Loan	www.virginmoneyus.com
Breus, Michael	Fall Asleep	www.soundsleepsolutions.com
Brown, Warren	Bake a Cake	www.cakelove.com
Carloftis, Jon	Garden	www.joncarloftis.com
Conti, Crazy Legs	Cure a Stomachache	www.crazylegsconti.com
Cooper, Tory L.	Plan a Wedding	www.torylcooper.com
Corcoran, Barbara	Sell a Home	www.barbaracorcoran.com
Cowie, Colin	Plan a Dinner Party	www.colincowie.com
Davis, Richard C.	Buy a House	www.trademark-properties.com
Deutschman, Alan	Make Life Changes	www.alandeutschman.com
Draper, Tim	Say No	www.dfj.com
Epperson, Sharon	Build Wealth	www.cnbc.com
Farley, Thomas P.	Mind Your Manners in a Fast-Paced World	www.newyorkinsider.tv
Fary, Lash	Find the Perfect Present	www.fabulousgifts.com
Feder, Erik	Find a Parking Spot	www.wheretofindparking.com
Fenton, Mark	Walk	www.markfenton.com
Fish, Joel	Concentrate	www.psychologyofsport.com
Garza, Jesse	Dress Slimmer	www.visual-therapy.com

McClanahan, Rue	Recover from a Breakup	www.expertsmedia.com
McGovern, Rob	Find and Land a Job	www.jobfox.com
Mercier, Laura	Apply Makeup	www.lauramercier.com
Messing, Barbara	Plan a Vacation	www.hotwire.com
Meyer, Laura	Remodel	www.remodelthis.net
Novak, Janice	Improve Your Posture	www.improveyourposture.com
Openshaw, Jennifer	Reduce Debt	www.themillionairezone.com
Ottusch, Lucinda	Do Laundry	www.whirlpoolinstituteoffabric science.com
Pasternak, Harley	Lose Weight	www.5factordiet.com
Peel, Kathy	File	www.familymanager.com
Peterson, Gunnar	Get in Shape	www.gunnarpeterson.com
Rios, Evette	Redecorate	www.evetterios.com
Rizzo, David	Commute	www.drroadmap.com
Rodan, Katie	Zap a Zit	www.rodanandfields.com
Roehm, Carolyne	Write Thank-You Notes	www.carolyneroehm.com
Rothbaum, Barbara Olasov	Overcome Fear	www.virtuallybetter.com
Schlereth, Mark	Recover from Surgery	www.markschlereth.com
Schwartz, Pepper	Sweep Someone off Their Feet	www.drpepperschwartz.com
Shine, Jimmy	Make Your Car Run	www.jimmyshine.com
Shubentsov, Yefim	Quit Smoking	www.expertsmedia.com
Shvo, Michael	Return Phone Calls	www.shvo.com
Solomon, Michael	Find a Lost Object	www.professorsolomon.com
Spindel, Janis	Find a Spouse	www.janisspindelmatchmaker.com
Starkey, Mary Louise	Clean Your Home	www.starkeyintl.com
Stephens, Robert	Make Your Computer Run Faster	www.geeksquad.com
St. John, Richard	Achieve Success	www.richardstjohn.com
Storm, Hannah	Get Ready in the Morning	www.hannahstorm.tv
Strauss, Neil	Make a Winning First Impression	www.neilstrauss.com
Taylor, Kent	Rake Leaves	www.nationalparksociety.com

Terry, Barbara	Change a Tire	www.barbaraterry.com
Trinka, Edwin	Make Someone Feel Good	www.expertsmedia.com
Trosko, John	Organize Your Closet	www.organizingla.com
Tsai, Ming	Chop Vegetables	www.ming.com
Underhill, Paco	Holiday Shop	www.envirosell.com
Unger, Zac	Wake Up	www.zacunger.com
Van Zandt, Clint	Find a Lost Child in a Crowd	www.livesecure.org
Vargas, Carlos	Stop Bleeding	www.expertsmedia.com
Vaynerchuk, Gary	Understand Wine	www.winelibrarytv.com
Walsh, Peter	Sort Mail	www.peterwalshdesign.com
Weeks, Samantha	Wade Through Information	www.thunderbirds.airforce.com
Wysong, James	Get Through Airport Security	www.franksteward.com
Yee, Rodney	Relax	www.yeeyoga.com
Zagnoni, Barbara	Iron	www.rowentausa.com
Zien, Sam	Cook a Meal	www.thecookingguy.com